READING POWER
AND STUDY SKILLS
FOR COLLEGE WORK

Carl A. Lefevre

Temple University

Helen E. Lefevre

Community College of Philadelphia

READING POWER AND STUDY SKILLS FOR COLLEGE WORK

HARCOURT BRACE JOVANOVICH, INC.

New York   San Diego   Chicago   San Francisco   Atlanta

ISBN: 0-15-575757-1

Library of Congress Catalog Card Number: 77-71229

Printed in the United States of America

Cover photo by Kenneth Karp

TO THE INSTRUCTOR

What reading skills are demanded of college students? What study skills are required?

This book is designed to provide not only an explanation of the various reading and study skills, but repeated practice as well. After the study skills work that opens the text, three stages of college textbook work are presented. Stage I covers mainly the acquisition of information; Stage II emphasizes both information and interpretation; Stage III provides the advanced reading that instructors may want to have available for a particular class or for individual students. The "Word Roundup" chapter gives students an overall acquaintance with dictionary and word study skills, and some practice in using them. The chapter entitled "Flexibility in College Reading" offers practice on a variety of college reading materials, and a chapter of library exercises comprises a planned approach to a student's actual use of the college library.

How can instructors cope with the difficulties many students have in reading college textbooks? This text takes two approaches to the problem. First, we begin with selections that present relatively few language difficulties; a good example is the earliest textbook passage, "Talking with the Body," on page 11. Our second approach involves the kind of question used in the exercises. A carefully planned series of questions leads students through a paragraph or a passage that might otherwise prove too difficult. The final question in an exercise sometimes requires the student to look back over a passage more thoughtfully or to write two or three sentences that answer an essay question. In our experience, these approaches are helpful in a college reading course. The Instructor's Manual that accompanies *Reading Power and Study Skills for College Work* discusses the various possibilities for a course based on this text.

We received a number of helpful suggestions for improving the presentation of the materials in this book from Professor Richard J. Smith of the University of Wisconsin at Milwaukee, Professor Paul B. Panes of Queensborough Community College, and Dr. Kenneth L. Carlson, Assistant Superintendent for Curriculum and Instruction in the Clio Area Schools, Clio, Michigan.

Mrs. Aimee Weis, Reference Librarian at the Community College of Philadelphia, also deserves special thanks for her many constructive suggestions concerning the "Library Skills" chapter.

TO THE STUDENT

The main purpose of this book is to strengthen your reading power; it will also help you with such college survival skills as outlining and note-taking. Whenever possible, a practice approach is used in addition to explanation. But first let's take an overall view of college work.

The most important job of your whole life may be the job you have right now—going to college. For most young people who go to college, this experience provides the basis for their adult lives. So college is important, now and later.

You are beginning a college semester. Your main task at the start is to plan your work for this particular semester, with its own special selection of courses. What do you need to know about each course in order to plan for it? First, study the course outline, or syllabus, and see what information it gives you. If there is no syllabus, your best approach is to ask the instructor what will be required in the course. There may be reading in addition to the textbook, for example, or there may be special projects or reports. Probably there will be major tests as well as shorter quizzes. Knowing what to expect will give you a basis for planning your work for the semester.

Some of your classmates are likely to take a negative attitude: the course is dumb, the teacher is dumb, the material is boring. These are really just excuses. That kind of thinking is not going to help a student succeed in college. Go your own way—take the course seriously.

Let's take another view of college work.

Students <u>learn</u> from these activities:	They are <u>judged</u> <u>and</u> <u>graded</u> on the basis of these activities:
Listening	Reciting in class
Reading	Taking objective tests
Taking notes	Writing essay answers on examinations
and	and sometimes
Studying	Doing special projects or writing reports

These activities involve a variety of skills, from listening well to writing essay answers on examinations. Chapter 1 of this book deals with the basic study skills. Other chapters give you practice with many kinds of reading.

Chapter 2, "Reading Power for College Textbooks," presents a variety of reading selections from various fields of study; it also includes some short passages that provide practice in understanding charts and other illustrative material. Chapter 3, "Word Roundup," is an introduction to college-level dictionary skills and word study. Chapter 4, "Flexibility in College Reading," contains samples of reading that demands special skills. And Chapter 5 gives you practical experience with college library skills.

Working with this textbook will introduce you to the principal reading and study skills you need for successful college work.

CONTENTS

Chapter 2   READING POWER FOR COLLEGE TEXTBOOKS

Chapter 2   READING POWER FOR COLLEGE TEXTBOOKS

Chapter 3   WORD ROUNDUP

Chapter 5   LIBRARY SKILLS

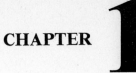

STUDY SKILLS FOR COLLEGE WORK

STUDY SKILLS FOR COLLEGE WORK

Students who enter college with poor or weak study habits have trouble managing their busy schedules. Let's consider the whole question of studying.

Study Habits and Methods

Good studying leads to good, solid learning. Study is a very important part of a student's preparation for recitation and for tests.

The habit of regular study may be hard to acquire. But it is absolutely necessary. If you have trouble finding a quiet place where you can concentrate, you might try studying in a library. Make yourself keep your mind on your work. This will take some self-discipline, especially at first. Every time you settle down to study, set yourself a definite task and plan how much work you will be able to get through before you've finished. Then, concentrate.

What does the word *study* mean? Study includes a variety of activities. If you have listened closely to the lectures, taken notes on them, and done your textbook reading carefully, you have an excellent groundwork for studying well. Choose the study methods that suit you best. You may want to focus on your lecture notes, with your text or textbook notes close at hand for easy reference. You may want to select important topics that appear both in the text and in lectures, and then write down the supporting points under these main headings. (This way, you're preparing for questions that may be asked on an examination.) You may want to ask yourself questions and recite, restating ideas and facts in your own words. Or you may want to study in a group, if you can find two or three other students who want to do so in a serious and organized way. When it is properly done, group study can reinforce your knowledge and build confidence.

Any course-related activity is a form of study. And studying well for one course teaches you how to study well for another.

Practice with Study Skills

Studying, note-taking, making outlines, taking objective tests, writing essay-type answers to exam questions—all these are important parts of your college work. The pages that follow are planned to give you practice in these skills.

This practice and the skills you will acquire should provide an added ingredient —confidence. Confidence in your ability to use these skills will help you as you open a textbook, listen to a lecture, or sit down to take a test.

Remember, though, that the only solid basis for successful college work is responsible, dependable, day-by-day attendance at class sessions, along with full attention in class and regular study habits.

You are aiming at success in what may be the most important experience of your life—going to college.

HOW ARE TEXTBOOKS ORGANIZED?

The chart below shows the usefulness of the various parts of a textbook. Not every text has all these parts, of course, but many do. Read the chart carefully, then review it.

This part of a textbook	*gives you this information:*
A. Title page	the general subject covered by the text and the name of the author
B. Copyright page	the copyright holder—the owner of the rights to the book; also, the date of first publication (plus other dates for later publication)
C. Preface or introduction	the overall purpose of the book and perhaps some suggestions for studying it
D. Table of contents	the organization and basic content of the text
E. Chapter title	the topic of the chapter
F. Chapter introduction	a survey of the chapter's content or an introductory explanation of it
G. Chapter subheadings	the specific points discussed under the overall topic of the chapter
H. Chapter conclusion	a summary of the chapter, or a final thought or conclusion
I. Charts, graphs, maps, pictures within the chapter	a clearer idea of some of the points that are discussed in the chapter
J. Footnotes or notes on sources	books or articles that are the source of specific quotations, ideas, or facts in the chapter; sometimes these "source notes" are at the bottom of the appropriate page (footnotes), and sometimes all together at the end of the chapter
K. Bibliography	titles of books and articles on related subjects; this may be at the end of each chapter or it may be in the back of the book
L. Study questions	help in reviewing the main points of the chapter
M. Glossary	meanings of specific terms
N. Appendix	additional information not included earlier, often in the form of tables or charts
O. Index	all the pages on which a particular topic, event, or person is discussed

EXERCISE 1 Checking on Textbook Organization

What part of a textbook would you turn to if you were looking for the kinds of information mentioned below?

Give a letter from the chart for your answer, that is, A for title page, and so on.

1. Some books or articles that will give you additional information _____

2. The main content of a chapter _____

3. The meaning of a special term _____

4. Within one chapter, a specific section or topic that you need to review _____

5. All the various references in the book to one famous author, or to one topic that you want to check _____

6. The location of a particular chapter somewhere in the book _____

7. The name of the author of the book _____

8. Some help in reviewing one important chapter _____

9. The main purpose of the book _____

10. A long table or chart that you believe is in the book somewhere _____

All these parts of a textbook are useful. One of the most useful is the *index*. If you're studying an American history text and need to brush up on the topic of the Supreme Court, check your index. It will tell you all the pages on which the Supreme Court is discussed.

APPROACHING A TEXTBOOK

Imagine this situation. You've bought the textbook for your Speech 101 course. Your professor has told you, rather offhandedly, "Buy it today and read the first chapter for tomorrow." You go home or to the library, and you sit down to read the chapter.

First, though, *first*—take a look at the book as a whole. Begin by checking the table of contents. Here it is. Read it; follow it carefully.

ORAL COMMUNICATION

EXERCISE 2   Examining a Table of Contents

1. This table of contents says quite a bit about the book. For example, the first section (Roman numeral I and letters A and B) tells you that the author regards speechmaking as just one part of a larger process, called

   _____

2. Under Roman numeral I, read the headings marked A and B. These two points probably will provide some motivation. That is, they will make you more interested in mastering communication skills. Can you suggest why? (Interpersonal relationships are those we have with other people.)

   _____

   _____

3. What two main kinds of speeches will you probably be making during your Speech 101 course?

   First _____

   Then_____

4. Which kind of speech evidently demands some serious library work?

   _____

5. At first, most of us are afraid or even terrified when we think of facing an audience and making a speech. In II, A, 1, 2, and 3, the author tells us how to *prepare* our first speeches.
       In what parts of the book does the author tell about the actual *delivery* of the speech—speaking to an audience? (Give Roman numeral, letter, and so on,

   as in the preceding sentence.) _____

6. What other part of the outline contains headings that suggest that speech skills can be useful to you in the future? (Give Roman numeral, etc.)

   _____

The table of contents of a textbook can give you a preview of the course you are about to take. Survey *the table of contents* and see each chapter as part of a whole learning experience. Keep this overall picture in mind as you progress through the book. It will take no time to do so, but is an attitude on your part that will pay off in greater learning.

FINDING MAIN IDEAS

As you read a textbook or listen to a lecture, your number one task is to discover the main ideas of the writer or speaker and the important points that are made to support each main idea.

The first part of a lecture or the first paragraphs of a chapter often give you a good idea of what lies ahead. The lecturer, for example, may say; "Today we'll discuss the causes of the Thirty Years War. The most important cause, of course, was . . ." Then you know that you'll hear a list of causes, with some supporting points explaining each one.

An outline shows the main ideas and supporting points or details very clearly. Let's look first at this paragraph.

> Good preparation for a speech is essential. First, you must select an appropriate topic, one that will interest your audience. Next, you need good, solid material to present—enough so that you are confident of your subject. You must also plan the order in which you can logically present your material. Finally, you must practice your speech.

Now look at page 6 and the "Preparation skills" listed under "II. The Informal Speech." Do you see how this part of the contents briefly outlines the same main idea and the same supporting points as the paragraph does?

Good notes can accomplish the same purpose as an outline. When taking notes, students often underline the main idea and then set the supporting points under it and farther to the right, as in an outline.

On the lines below, follow this method. Underline your main idea and set your supporting points in to the right, as the lines show. Take your notes on the speech paragraph above. Work slowly and carefully.

_____

_____

_____

_____

_____

Examine the notes you've just taken. If you did a careful job, you have notes that show a main idea and four supporting points. They are also notes that will be easy to understand when you review.

Taking good notes and making a good outline—these are valuable study skills.

TEXTBOOKS AND LECTURES: OUTLINING
AND NOTE-TAKING

The table of contents of *Oral Communication* on page 6 shows you the general approach and overall outline of an entire book. When you have to submit a term report for your sociology or English course, you will need a really good outline before you start to write. Then you'll know how to begin your paper and where to go from there. Your speech teacher may demand a careful outline for each speech. And students sometimes outline their lectures or textbook chapters.

But not all lectures or chapters lend themselves to outlining. Neat and careful notes are just as useful for study purposes, especially if they resemble an outline in form.

When you are studying a textbook chapter, your purpose in either outlining or note-taking is the same: to master the material in the chapter, to fix it in your mind *in an orderly way*. You are also preparing for review.

The orderly form of an outline makes the main points clear and shows the items that support or illustrate each main point.

Orderly note-taking does the same things. An underlined heading, such as Human communication, might have two points under it, like this:

Human communication

—for developing human relationships
—for personal growth and maturity

Compare these notes with I, A and B on page 6.

So you see that *orderly notes*, whether of lectures or of textbook chapters, *have much in common with outlines*.

In the next short section you will practice some simple outlining and orderly note-taking.

Outlining and Note-Taking

Generally it is best to read a section of a textbook chapter, then go back and review. This is a good time to review, before going on to read the rest of the chapter.

Below is a section from a speech text, *The New American Speech*, by Wilhelmina G. Hedde. (It corresponds to the section in the outline on page 6 labeled II, B, 4, "Talking with the body.") As a first step, *read the passage through*. For your first reading, ignore the numbers and letters in the margin.

TALKING WITH THE BODY

[1]We do not talk only with the vocal cords, throat or mouth.

I. We talk all over, with the whole body. Good talkers tend to have

A. lively bodies. They lean forward or backward according to their mood, shrug their shoulders, move the body, nod the head, lift the eyebrows, and tell us how

B. they feel about things by their facial expressions. Their hands are seldom still for more than a few seconds at a time, and even the legs and feet are usually active. Persons with a lively voice usually also have a lively body.

[2]Likewise, the person with a dull, dead voice more often has an inert body. Such a person is uninteresting all over. To tell the truth, people cannot be divided into pigeonholes, with one pigeonhole called "voice," another "body," and still another "mind." We are alert or inert, interesting or dull, not in one pigeonhole or another, but all over. We live all over. We think all over. We talk all over.

II. *How Talking with the Body Carries Meanings to Listeners*

[3]Before the speaker utters a word, he or she begins to carry meanings to all who are watching. Let us see how this is done.

A.   [4]The eye is quicker than the ear. The moment a speaker comes to the platform, his or her manner tells the audience something. The speaker may shuffle, stride belligerently, or walk in a quiet, purposeful manner. The audience can sense at once the meaning conveyed by an approach. While talking, the speaker continues to carry fine shades of meaning to the audience by moving about, shifting weight, twisting and turning, punctuating or interrupting the words by movements of the shoulders, hands, head, and even the eyebrows. These meanings are caught instantly by the audience, whereas the ideas expressed by the speaker's words unfold themselves more slowly.

B.   [5]People looking at a speaker tend to imitate the speaker's movements. They do this unconsciously, of course, but they do it unfailingly. They do it not only with speakers, but with all types of performers. If a football player carries the ball to the left, spectators sway visibly to the left. If a squad of sprinters comes thundering down the track, the audience leaps to its feet—upright like

1. the sprinters. These are movements visible to the eye; but even when the eye cannot see, this imitation goes on. In a play, for example, if one of the characters stands erect, bold, and defiant, members of the audience will feel

From *The New American Speech* by Wilhelmina G. Hedde. Reprinted by permission of J. B. Lippincott Company.

the pull to sit slightly more erect than before. If, later, another character sits drooped and dejected, the audience will feel the downward pull of the drooping posture. Even though members of the audience seldom outwardly change their

2. posture, the <u>inner pull</u> is there. Always they are imitating inwardly what they see.

C.   [6]<u>What this means to the speaker, reader, or actor</u>. When you are talking, therefore, your bodily action will do one of three things to those who listen.

1. If you use no action, or almost none, the audience will relax too much, or even become drowsy. It cannot give close attention to what you say.
2. If you fidget and fumble, the audience inwardly will fidget and fumble too. This will make some persons outright nervous or irritated, and it will distract everyone from what you are saying.
3. If you have controlled action, and enough of it, the audience will be kept aroused and alert. Such an audience will find it easier to pay attention.

[7]In other words, it is never a question of whether we will talk with our body or not; it is only a question of what kind of talking we will do.

III. *How Talking with the Body Aids the Speaker*

[8]One who tries to talk only with the voice—without using the whole body— is literally not a whole person. Such an individual is unable either to think efficiently or to talk effectively. You think, not only with the brain, but with the whole body—brain, nerves, muscles, glands, and all. So when you see speakers who fidget and fumble, scratch their faces, jerk their feet, and twist their fingers, you can know that they are not doing a very good job of thinking.

A.   [9]<u>Freedom from nervousness depends on control of muscles</u>. Do you feel nervous while speaking in public? Well, don't think you're the only one. Every beginning student is nervous—afraid of the audience, afraid of being laughed at by other students. The breath becomes spasmodic, the knees shake, the hands twitch, and at times even the teeth chatter. This, you understand, is the *normal* behavior of beginning speakers. (Experienced speakers are nervous, too, but some have learned to control and conceal it.)

B.   [10]Now, what is nervousness? It is simply muscular tension. And <u>this muscular tension demands an outlet through bodily action</u>.

[11]Suppose you try to suppress action while speaking. You are going to speak without moving at all. Very well, try it! You cannot do it any more than you can fly, for down inside you little nervous explosions take place, somewhat like the explosions from a steam valve when there is too much pressure. These explosions make you fidget and jerk, twist a handkerchief, button and unbutton your coat, chew your fingernails, rock up and down on your toes—anything to drain off the excess tension. Your unhappy audience, of course, is inwardly imitating every jerk and twitch, very much to its discomfort; but you cannot think of them. In fact, you cannot think effectively of anything for the time being, for you do not have control of your whole body.

[12]This is stage fright, and we have all been afflicted by it. How can we overcome it? Of course, there is no royal cure, but there is a way by which

C. you learn to control it. <u>Relax and control your muscles by using them</u>.

EXERCISE 3   Outlining a Textbook Chapter

Look back at "Talking with the Body" and see how the underlined sentences and phrases next to the numbers and letters in the margin fit into a kind of outline. Use them to make a topic outline of the passage.

A topic outline like the one on page 6 does not use complete sentences. When a whole sentence in the passage is underlined, change it. For example, the first underlined sentence could become "Talking with the whole body." (Notice—one capital letter only.)

Work slowly and carefully as you make your outline. Careful work is important.

    I. _____

       A. _____

       B. _____

    II. _____

       A. _____

       B. _____

           1. _____

           2. _____

       C. _____

           1. _____

           2. _____

           3. _____

    III. _____

       A. _____

       B. _____

       C. _____

Now study your outline. Does it give you the main ideas and supporting points of the passage? Note how the supporting points fit in a logical way under their headings. "Lively bodies" and "facial expressions" are two ways of "Talking with the whole body." That is the secret of outlining or of note-taking—showing your main ideas, and under those headings showing your supporting points.

Name_____ Date_____

The Note-Taking Approach

Outlining is not always easy. Often, when studying a textbook or listening to a lecture, note-taking of a less formal kind is more dependable. But you should always try to make your notes look a bit like an outline.

For example, the part of your outline of "Talking with the Body" that includes II, A, B, and C, might look like this in note form.

How talking with the body carries meanings to listeners
 —bodily poise or nervousness shows even before you begin to talk
 —audience imitates speaker's movements
  actual physical response
  or inner pull
 —what this means
  no action; aud. drowsy
  too much action; aud. distracted
  controlled action; aud. alert

Notes like these are easy to review. If you keep trying to organize your notes on texts and lectures, you will soon learn this useful skill. Some students make a point of recopying their notes in order to get them better organized, until they have learned to organize the notes as they take them.

EXERCISE 4   Taking Notes on a Textbook Chapter

On the lines below, take notes as seems best to you for the third part (III, A, B, and C) of "Talking with the Body."

_____

_____

_____

_____

_____

As you listen to each lecture in your subject-matter courses, try to take organized notes. It's one of the most useful college skills. If the teacher brings in something on a subject other than the one he or she is lecturing on, leave it out—or perhaps put it in, in parentheses.

 Taking organized notes *as you listen* will help you organize your thoughts *as you read.*

15

THE ART OF LISTENING

Have you ever thought about *organized listening*? One of your first new experiences in college probably will be a lecture by one of your instructors. Be prepared to listen in an organized way. As you listen for the main points being made, take notes that will show which points are the big, general ideas and which are the ones that fit under these headings. Underline the important points, or print them in capital letters—whatever suits you. After class, look over your notes and fill in any empty spaces from memory. Or ask a classmate. Some students recopy their notes between lectures; this is a real learning experience. Before the next class, look over your notes from the previous lecture. This takes just a few minutes, but it's a wonderful investment of time. As class opens, ask yourself whether the instructor is continuing with the same topic as last time or is starting on another.

Learning to listen in an organized way, and to take organized notes, will increase your listening power and your learning power.

EXERCISE 5   Listening Practice I

For your first listening practice, ask someone to read you the passage on pages 11–12 called "Talking with the Body." While you listen, take notes as though you were at a lecture. Space is provided for your notes on page 18.

In taking your notes, try to use headings for the main ideas. Place supporting points under these headings.

Here's one hint: after the introduction, there are two main parts in the passage, one telling how talking with the body helps *listeners*, the other telling how talking with the body helps the *speaker*.

EXERCISE 6   Listening Practice II

For further practice, ask someone to read you the passage on the Bill of Rights on page 31. Take careful notes. Space is provided on page 18.

When you've finished your notes, check to see that you have included the main provisions of the Bill of Rights and the other amendments mentioned in the passage, and also the question of their effectiveness today.

Other Listening Practice

For additional practice, ask a classmate or friend to read you any of the textbook paragraphs or passages in the second chapter of this book. Repeat this from time to time until you feel that you no longer need the practice.

Listening Practice I: Notes

_____

_____

_____

_____

_____

_____

_____

_____

Listening Practice II: Notes

_____

_____

_____

_____

_____

_____

_____

_____

Remember, continue your listening practice until you feel that you no longer need it.

TAKING TESTS

Tests are important. So are test grades.

Other things do count, such as oral presentations and term reports. Some teachers take account of class recitation when figuring out a grade, and your final grade in certain courses may depend to quite an extent on your term paper. But grades in general tend to be based on tests.

Your Grade Point Average (GPA) will determine your standing in your class. And if you want to transfer to another college, you may find that to the admissions officer you are more a GPA than anything else. To earn a good GPA, you must learn how to take tests.

Some basically good students have trouble with tests. Two causes of this are nervousness over taking a test, and lack of knowledge of the techniques or tricks of taking tests. Of special importance is knowing how to write an essay-type answer on an examination.

Practice in note-taking and in test techniques should build your confidence and help you to answer different kinds of test questions. Remember that college tests are harder than those in high school. A midterm exam may require you to answer quickly a number of objective questions plus an essay question or two—all in one fifty-minute period. A college final can last two or three hours and demand a lot in the way of good skills and solid information.

Your examination may be all objective, all essay questions or problems (as in math), or a combination of both. For the exam, you need to have in mind both the overall ideas or concepts of the course and the supporting skills or facts. If you have prepared carefully, and if you know how to go about taking a test, you've done all you can.

Look at the next page for some general hints on taking tests, followed by a few tips on answering objective questions.

As you read them, ask yourself whether each bit of advice is something that *you* need to remember.

Taking Tests: Some Hints

1. Arrive a minute early. Dispose of your books and other belongings. Have your pen or pencil ready and be all set to start the moment the test is handed out.

2. Read the directions carefully—twice if necessary. If you still don't understand, go quietly to the instructor and ask for help in a low, polite voice.

3. Look the test over, so that you can plan your time.

4. Begin work in a businesslike way, not in too much of a hurry. Do your best, but don't expect to have a perfect paper. Probably no one will.

5. If a question stumps you, make a little mark beside it in the margin and leave it. You can come back to it later.

Now go ahead and answer the questions you know. This will build your confidence, and you're more likely to remember things you've forgotten. Finish the test, answering all the questions that are fairly easy for you. Then go back and have a try at those you've left out. You might earn some credit even for a poor answer.

6. Don't ask for or give help. Cheating or what might look like cheating can have serious results. If your pen is out of ink, speak to the teacher, not to the student next to you. The smallest suggestion of cheating could count against you.

7. Do *not* be in a rush to leave, even if others go. Take time to check over your paper.

Answering Objective Questions

1. When you're not sure of the right answer, take a chance and guess, as a general rule. (But if there's a penalty for wrong answers, don't guess.)

2. Watch out for statements in true-false or multiple-choice questions that have words such as *not, some, most, very,* or *often*. They affect the meaning of the sentence.

Double negatives are tricky; "the idea was not unattractive" means that the idea was attractive.

3. In answering multiple-choice questions, cross out the choices you're sure are wrong, and concentrate on the ones that are left.

4. In answering matching questions, lightly cross out the items you've already used. Lightly—because you may change your mind.

5. Read true-false questions very carefully. Remember that a single word such as *seldom* or *usually* can change the meaning of a statement, and if any part of it is false, the whole statement is false.

6. You may be asked to fill in blanks in a sentence. Be careful; after filling in the blank, reread the whole sentence just to be sure. Short-answer questions are similar; always reread the question and your answer.

EXERCISE 7 Practice with an Objective Test on "Talking with the Body"

In college, a reading assignment generally has some kind of follow-up. Usually this is a quiz or test. Such a quiz may consist of true-false questions, probably ten or twenty of them.

Now for some true-false questions on "Talking with the Body" (pages 11–12). Remember that a *false* item may contain words from the passage that make it *sound* right. For this first practice, the righthand column gives you the number of the paragraph that tells whether the statement is true or false. Mark T or F in the blank before each statement.

Paragraph

1. _____ We think only with the brain, but we talk all over.   8

2. _____ Audiences can tell a lot about speakers by their bodily approach.   3, 4

3. _____ People can be sorted into pigeonholes, with one pigeonhole called "voice," another "body," and still another "mind."   2

4. _____ People in an audience may not move, but they feel a pull on their muscles as they listen to a speaker and see his or her movements.   5

5. _____ Even the eyebrows can carry fine shades of meaning.   4

6. _____ If you use too much action, the audience will be drowsy and cannot give close attention to what you say.   6

7. _____ A speaker who tries to talk only with the voice is able to think efficiently and talk effectively.   8

8. _____ It is normal for beginning speakers to be nervous.   9

9. _____ Some experienced speakers have learned to control and conceal their nervousness.   9

10. _____ You should relax and control your muscles so that you can speak without moving your body.   11, 12

Some of these statements are false because of *one* word. See if you can spot two of these.

A. In number 3 the word _____ should be _____

B. In number 6 the word _____ should be _____

PLANET, STAR, GALAXY, UNIVERSE

We'll use the following passage as the basis for some practice with three kinds of objective questions: true-false, multiple-choice, and fill-in. First note the vocabulary items; then read the passage carefully.

galaxy a group of millions of stars
meteorites defined for you in the passage
a mortal a human being

planetoid a minor planet
satellite a small planet revolving around a larger one; a moon
solar pertaining to the sun

When we think of the planet earth, on which we live, we often think of it as one part of the solar system. This solar system includes eight other planets, for example, Mars, Venus, and Jupiter, the largest planet. The system also includes many planetoids, and other matter such as comets and meteors. The center of the entire system is a medium-sized, medium-hot star that we call the sun. In other words, we live on a planet revolving around a star. To us, this sun-centered system seems immense. Man has already traveled from the earth to its satellite, the moon, but the other planets within the solar system are very distant. Do you think you or I will ever set foot on Mars?

As residents of a planet within the solar system, we sometimes ask ourselves, "How old is the solar system? When did it take shape? How long ago?"

Over the past centuries, the earth has been struck by meteorites, which are fragments from other parts of the solar system. From various measurements, scientists have been able to estimate the age of these meteorites as four and a half billion years. So at present the best guess as to the age of the solar system is 4.5 billion years. No earth rock that old has been found.

Our solar system is only a very small part of the galaxy called the Milky Way. This galaxy is a star system containing millions of stars, many larger than the star which is our sun. As we look into the sky on a clear night, we see many of the other stars in the Milky Way. And the Milky Way is only one among an indefinite number of galaxies in the vast universe in which we live. It is difficult or impossible for a mere mortal to imagine the great extent of the universe around us.

Yet on one minor planet, the earth, circling around an average star among the millions in just one galaxy—on this minor planet, there exist human beings who are asking questions about the entire universe. We are possibly the only askers of questions in the universe.

The age of the solar system, in fact the age of the universe, is one question that will continue to be asked. How old is our universe? How long will it endure? We may never have a clear answer.

Why not reread the passage before attempting to answer the questions on the opposite page? As you read, *think* about what the passage tells you.

EXERCISE 8   Practice with an Objective Test on "Planet, Star, Galaxy, Universe"

Work slowly and carefully.

Multiple-choice. Write the letter of the correct statement in the space given.

1. A. The four words of the title begin with the smallest, and end with the largest part of what exists around us.
   B. The four words begin with the largest and end with the smallest part.
   C. The four parts named are equal in size.   *Which, A, B, or C?*   _____

2. A. The age of the meteorites has not been studied.
   B. The age of the meteorites is established as 4.5 billion years.
   C. The age of the meteorites has been estimated as 4.5 billion years.   _____

3. Careful with this one.
   A. In the near future we will know the age of the solar system and the universe.
   B. We may never know the age of the solar system and the universe.
   C. Modern science has determined the age of the solar system and of the universe.   _____

True-false. Mark each statement T or F.

4. We dwellers on earth are undoubtedly the only askers of questions in the universe.   _____

5. Meteorites, which sometimes strike the earth and then can be studied by scientists, come from other parts of the solar system.   _____

6. Our sun is a medium-sized, medium-hot planet.   _____

Fill-in. Neatly write in the word or words needed.

7. Our earth is a _____, one of nine major ones revolving around the sun.

8. The sun is one _____ among millions in the Milky Way.

9. The Milky Way is a _____, a word that can be defined as

   _____

10. There are an indefinite number of such groups of stars in the _____ around us.

Go back and check over your answers slowly and with care. Some of the true-false statements are false because of one word.

11. The word that is wrong in number _____ is _____

12. The word that is wrong in number _____ is _____

Hints on Answering Essay Questions

Essay questions are particularly important. Why?

Well, for one thing, they usually count more than objective questions do. On a midterm, you might have twenty objective questions, each counting 3 points. Total: 60 points. Then you might have two essay questions, each counting 20 points. Some essay questions count 30 or 40 points out of 100.

Another reason they're important is that in using essay questions your instructor is often testing your understanding of the basic ideas or subject matter of the course.

As a first step, read—no, *study!*—these general hints on answering essay questions.

1. Read all the questions first. If you are allowed to answer only two out of three, or three out of four, make your choice and cross out the other. Now concentrate on the ones you've chosen. Be sure you understand them.

2. If some questions count more than others, plan your time accordingly.

3. You may feel that you know quite a bit about the subject of the question. But remember that what you know must be *clearly expressed* on your test paper. Vague, rambling statements won't count for much.

4. Organizing your answer is important. You may want to jot down some points and then number them to show the order in which you will use them. The one you wrote down last might be the best to start with.

5. Don't pad your answers. Give just the main ideas and supporting points that fit the question. Include only material that answers the particular question you are working on. Look back at the question if you need to.

6. At the end of each answer, leave some blank space on your paper or in your bluebook. You may want to add something later.

7. Be sure you've numbered your answers properly and that you've answered every question. Even a poor answer may earn some credit.

8. Write neatly and clearly. Handwriting need not be beautiful to be clear. Your teacher will react positively to a neat paper, whether consciously or unconsciously.

Don't think this is kindergarten stuff. It's important in college.

9. When you have finished, read over your paper with care. Neatly cross out any words you don't want.

10. You can use a caret (∧) to insert an extra word or two in a sentence. But do this as legibly as you can.

Basic Method of Answering Essay Questions

Let's suppose you are taking a test. You have read the test through, have answered all the objective questions, and are ready to start on the essay questions. You have the general hints on the preceding page pretty well in mind.

Now—how do you start?

One authority, Dr. Leslie Nason, has said, "Students should be careful to answer each question precisely in the very first sentences. Illustrations, examples, and further discussion should be included only after the question has been answered directly."

In other words, first make a general statement answering the question, then support your statement with facts, examples, analysis.

Make a statement—support your statement. This is a good way of planning a paragraph, and certainly a good way to go about answering an essay question.

One technique that often is useful is to include in the general statement some echo of the question. Repeat a word or two of it.

If you are asked to explain the three main causes of the Korean War, for example, you could open the three parts of your answer by saying "The first main cause of the Korean War was . . ." and "The second main cause of this war . . ." and "The third cause . . ." Your teacher will see that you have the question clearly in mind and will find it easy to follow your answer. Clear organization pays off in points earned.

In general it's best to present your answer in one solid paragraph, unless there's a good reason to use more. For the question on the Korean War, you could use three paragraphs, one for each cause.

We will practice the general-statement-plus-support method of answering essay questions. As our basis we'll use a short passage dealing with an American slaveholder on page 28. But first we'll review the terms that instructors often use in asking essay-type exam questions.

Terms Used in Essay-Type Exams

Study the meanings of these terms that are often used in examination questions.

compare   give resemblances or similarities—points that are alike

contrast   give differences

criticize   judge the value of something, whether positive or negative

define   state the exact meaning; often, give the general class to which the thing belongs and then its special qualities ("A dictionary is a *book* that gives definitions of words.")

describe   give an account of the appearance of something or of a process or event

diagram   make a drawing or sketch, adding labels if necessary

discuss   look at both sides of a question (sometimes used to mean *explain*)

enumerate   list

evaluate   tell what's good or bad about an object, event, or process

explain   give a clear statement, usually telling *how* or *why*

identify   tell *who* or *what* is referred to, often adding *when* or *where*

illustrate   give examples, real or imaginary; in an art course, possibly draw a picture

justify   show the reasons why something was done

outline   present a clearly organized answer including main points and supporting material

prove   show that something is true by presenting factual or experimental evidence or by logic

review   in an organized way, give an account of something; similar to *outline*

state   give the facts or main points clearly and briefly; sometimes means *list*

summarize   present in short form the main facts or events and the main supporting information; similar to *outline* and *review*

trace   briefly give the main sequence of facts or events, in time order; usually used concerning the development of a trend or with regard to a series of events leading up to some major event

analyze is another word used occasionally in questions. To analyze is to examine the various parts or the basic nature of something. We analyze our feelings, or a situation, or one aspect of a situation—for example, its potential for violence.

These terms are sometimes used a bit loosely. An instructor might ask you to *outline, review, describe, discuss, explain, review, summarize,* or *trace* the events leading up to the American Revolution.

EXERCISE 9   Using Essay-Type Examination Terms

Here is a series of testing situations. Put yourself in the place of the instructor. Which word would you use? Try to select the *best* word for each question. The first answer is given, as an example.

1. A music teacher wants the class to show that they understand clearly the meaning of some special terms used in music.   *define*

2. A literature instructor wants students to demonstrate their understanding of the similarities in two poems written at different times and places.

3. In a home economics class, the students are to tell the difference between the effects of using a wire whisk and an ordinary eggbeater.

4. A political science teacher wants the class to give a sympathetic version of why the United States sent troops into a certain country.

5. Next, the students are asked to give an objective or unsympathetic view of this same event.

6. Music students are asked to give various points of view concerning the contribution of jazz to modern music.

7. A Shakespeare instructor wants students to present a clear picture of the construction of the Elizabethan stage.

8. A history teacher asks the class to show they understand the main stages in the development of industrial power in England.

9. Students in an art class are assigned a painting by another member of the class; they must tell its strengths and weaknesses.

10. A class in American history is asked to present briefly an account of Lincoln's political views.

11. Students are given a list of names of people and places; they are asked to tell who or what these names represent.

12. A literature instructor wants students to give the titles of poems by Keats that show Keats's love of nature.

13. A sociology teacher asks the class to give a thoughtful statement concerning the role of television in the lives of preschool children.

AN AMERICAN SLAVEHOLDER

In this passage concerning a famous early American who was a slaveowner, notice as you read that the passage has two themes: (1) what he tried to do for his slaves; (2) his problems in connection with freeing them.

[1]During wartime, Americans become more mobile than usual. And during the American Revolution, one high-ranking officer from Virginia fought in Pennsylvania and other northern states. He had grown up with slavery, was a slaveholder himself, and had never thought of slavery as a problem. Yet as he traveled through the free states, he noted with surprise, then with admiration and envy, that these states did not base their economic life on slavery. Being dependent on slave labor, he concluded, was "a misfortune."

[2]Somewhat later he wrote to a close friend this view of his own role as a slaveholder:

The unfortunate condition of the persons whose labors I in part employed has been the only unavoidable source of regret. To make the adults among them as easy and comfortable as their actual state of ignorance would admit; and to lay a foundation to prepare the rising generation for a destiny different from that in which they were born, afforded some satisfaction to my mind, and could not, I hoped, be displeasing to the justice of the Creator.

The writer of this letter was George Washington.

[3]In 1797, as Washington prepared to return to Virginia after his service as president, he quietly left behind him in Pennsylvania a number of his slaves. After six months in this state, as he knew, these people would automatically become free under Pennsylvania law.

[4]Back at Mt. Vernon, however, slave marriages were a problem. Washington, unlike many slaveholders, had for years encouraged legal marriages among slaves. His own slaves had intermarried freely with his wife's slaves, who were part of her estate and could not legally be freed by him. If he freed his own slaves, their husbands or wives, and children, would still be bound in slavery.

[5]By 1799, Washington was supporting many more slaves than he could usefully employ in his farming system. Yet he would neither sell them nor hire them out to others, since he knew that either way they might be treated badly or even brutally. And in 1799 he could no longer postpone making his will. His decision, the best he could come up with, was to free his slaves "on the decease of my wife," Martha. She was frail and older than he, likely to die soon. He would inherit her estate, and all the slaves could be freed.

[6]But in 1799 it was Washington himself who died. Martha inherited her late husband's slaves—all waiting for her death, and their freedom. She also had slaves of her own. Quickly she made her decision: she freed them all. And so that problem was solved.

[7]Washington had specified in his will that his older slaves were to be cared for in their old age, and his heirs paid pensions to them for more than thirty years. He had left money for the education of the children, but these plans were soon crushed. His fellow Virginians passed laws forbidding the education of blacks. Washington did not live to see this sad event.

Name_____ Date_____

EXERCISE 10 Selecting Material That Answers an Essay Question

One important kind of reading you do in college is reading the questions on tests. Here's your essay question on "An American Slaveholder." Read it with care.

   Was Washington's treatment of his slaves generally good or bad? Explain.

Begin your answer with a statement saying that Washington's treatment of his slaves was generally good, since that's what the passage tells us. Then support this statement. There are two "treatment" items in the letter quoted in paragraph 2; one in paragraph 4; one in 5; two in 7. Points on *freedom* appear also, but leave them out! Your question deals with *treatment*.

   Answer the question in one solid paragraph. Remember to start with a general statement on Washington's treatment of his slaves.

THE BILL OF RIGHTS

It was the year 1789. In America a new nation was being born. Two years earlier, in Philadelphia, delegates from the colonies had labored to draw up a Constitution for the United States of America.

In the Constitution produced in Philadelphia, some guarantees of civil rights were provided, but many citizens were not at all satisfied. More guarantees were needed to protect the individual against a government which might become arbitrary and tyrannical, they insisted. In 1789 James Madison introduced a group of amendments, ten of which were ratified promptly. The First Amendment alone guarantees religious freedom, freedom of speech and the press, and the right of peaceful assemblage. The first ten amendments to the Constitution have traditionally been called the Bill of Rights.

Over the years other amendments have been added, with fuller guarantees: the Thirteenth, which abolished slavery, and the Fifteenth and the Nineteenth, which guaranteed the right to vote regardless of race, sex, or previous condition of servitude. Another great addition to the Bill of Rights was the Fourteenth, an amendment which denied the right of any state to deprive any person of life, liberty, or property without due process of law. This amendment stated the important principle of the equal protection of the law for every individual without exception.

Are all these guarantees in full effect today? We know they are not. Equal protection of the law? Not always.

What every American must keep in mind is that the civil rights of each of us depend on the civil rights of every American citizen, whether white or black, male or female, poor or rich, educated or uneducated. When the lawful rights of any citizen are denied, all of us are in danger. My civil rights—your civil rights—are equally in danger.

EXERCISE 11 Answering an Essay Question on "The Bill of Rights"

In studying American history, political science, or sociology, you will find concern for civil rights. After you have studied the five paragraphs on page 31, a teacher might ask you to show your understanding of the passage by writing one paragraph of your own. The question might be:

> Discuss the rights and protections that *you* as an American citizen have under the Bill of Rights and other amendments to the Constitution.

Begin your answer with a general statement echoing the question, something like this: "The Bill of Rights and other amendments give me broad personal freedoms and protection against arbitrary acts of police or government." Then go on, in the rest of your paragraph, to mention specific rights and protections. (Remember, neatness makes a good impression.)

_____

_____

_____

_____

_____

_____

_____

_____

_____

_____

_____

_____

THE MAGNA CARTA

In the five paragraphs below, words and phrases are underlined here and there to help you make the outline asked for on the opposite page. (The word *magna* in the title means "great" and *carta* means "charter"—that is, "great charter.")

[1]In the year 1200 a new king, John, sat on the throne of England. And in 1200 the English throne was strong. The king had <u>absolute power</u> over his barons and the common people. He could condemn any man to <u>exile or imprisonment</u>, and even, if he chose, to <u>death</u>. In addition to having power in England, he was strong in France. England had been at war with France for years, and great provinces of that country were under his rule.

[2]Gradually, the <u>destruction of John's power</u> was brought about by his own <u>greed and cruelty</u>, and also by <u>many misdeeds</u>, such as causing the murder of a baron who was his own nephew. He angered his barons by marrying a very wealthy heiress who was solemnly pledged to one of them. Furthermore, he taxed his barons unmercifully, seized their property at will, and treated them with contempt. A final offense was the <u>loss of the war with France</u>. National pride was crushed.

[3]Almost inevitable was the <u>rebellion of the barons</u> against such a king. In January of 1215, a group of his most powerful barons confronted him. They demanded guarantees against arbitrary arrest, imprisonment without cause, exile, seizure of lands, and sudden special taxes. King John had no intention of granting any of their demands. Instead, he pretended to bargain and meanwhile began to strengthen his military position by bringing in hired troops from abroad. In order to avoid armed conflict, the barons talked with the officers and leading citizens of London, all of whom hated John. In May came the peaceful <u>occupation of London and defeat of John</u>.

[4]Now John had no choice. Though king of England, he was forced— much against his will—to submit to the rule of law. In the end, he had to grant to his subjects the charter of liberties known as the <u>Magna Carta of 1215</u>. Here are two key <u>guarantees against arbitrary acts</u> of the king:

    39. No free man may be seized, or imprisoned, or dispossessed, or exiled . . . nor will we go against him or send against him except by the legal judgment of his peers and by the law of the land.

    40. To no one will we sell, to no one will we deny or delay, right and justice.

The basic guarantees of the Magna Carta were reaffirmed over and over again, willingly or unwillingly, by English kings in the centuries that followed. The <u>rule of law</u> established in the charter endured in spite of their opposition. From time to time the barons gathered in meetings called parliaments or talk-fests. These <u>talk-fests of the barons, held to discuss their rights</u> and interests, helped to maintain these rights.

[5]Thus there was established in England the great principle of rule by law, not by men. Out of the informal parliaments or talk-fests there gradually developed over the centuries the <u>English Parliament, now the cornerstone of English government</u>.

Name _____ Date _____

EXERCISE 12 Outlining "The Magna Carta"

To help you with your outline, two main headings are given. Also, at the left are the paragraph and line numbers that tell you where to look for the underlined items you need (the numerals 1, 2 mean paragraph 1, line 2, and so on). Rephrase the items as you choose. Remember to capitalize the first word in each item. *Write clearly and neatly.*

I. John as king of England

1, 2   A. _____

1, 4   1. _____

1, 4   2. _____

2, 1   B. _____

2, 2   1. _____

2, 7   2. _____

II. Development of the rule of law

3, 1   A. _____

3, 9–10   B. _____

4, 3–4   C. _____

4, 4   1. _____

4, 12   2. _____

4, 14–15   D. _____

_____

5, 3–4   E. _____

_____

Important: Read over your outline. (1) See how it gives you the main points of the passage. (2) See how each item fits under its heading—study this.

    Notice that this outline was made easy for you. Usually, when taking orderly notes or outlining, you'll have to figure things out for yourself. However, *studying this and the outline on page 6 will help you to develop outlining skill.*

EXERCISE 13   Answering Objective Questions on "The Magna Carta"

Try to answer the questions below without looking back at the passage on page 34.

Mark each of the following three statements T or F, for true or false.

1. The talk-fests of the barons gradually developed into the English
   Parliament of today.   _____

2. Once the Magna Carta was signed, English rights were completely safe.   _____

3. The barons had no real need to hold their talk-fests.   _____

Give a short answer to each of the next three questions.

4. Why did John marry a woman who was engaged to one of his barons?

   _____

5. What would make you think that John expected armed conflict with the barons?

   _____

6. After 1215, by what method could the king have a baron put in prison?

   _____

Match the following items by writing the correct letter in the space provided.

7. How John destroyed his own power _____   a. Rule of law

8. The Magna Carta _____   b. Rule by men, not law

9. English kings, including John _____   c. Misdeeds, loss of war with
                                                    France

Check over this exercise before going on to the essay question.

Here is some space for notes on the essay question on page 39. Pay attention to
the order of your notes. You might number them to show the order in which you want
to use them.

   _____   _____

   _____   _____

   _____   _____

EXERCISE 14   Answering an Essay Question on "The Magna Carta"

If you can, answer the essay question below without looking back at the passage on the Magna Carta. But study the passage carefully if you need to. Here's your question:

> What do you think John was like personally? Some of his personal qualities are mentioned in the passage. Others we must judge by what he did at various times. Was, he, for example, wise or foolish, overall? Did he show any signs of being clever? Was he, do you think, stubborn or reasonable?

Answer this question in one carefully written paragraph.

Always, check your paper. Use a caret (∧) to add a word or phrase if you need to.

SKIMMING

Skimming enables an expert reader to cover a great deal of material in a short time. Even for the expert, however, skimming does not work for science or math materials. It will not help you to remember details in your study reading, or to appreciate the literary quality of poems and stories.

Most of us use skimming only in special ways.

When Is Skimming Appropriate?

Skimming is excellent for surveying material before you really read it—for example, a textbook chapter. Look at the title, the introduction, the headings and subheadings, and the conclusion. Then go back and *study* the chapter.

When you are interested in only certain kinds of information, skim over what doesn't interest you. Then study carefully or make notes on the information you are after.

If you're looking for specific information in a book, check the table of contents and the index to locate the pages where the information is likely to be found. Skim those pages to find the specific information you want.

Suppose I Have Just Enough Time to Skim a Chapter or an Article?

If you find yourself in a situation where you don't have enough time to do your assigned reading, follow the survey-skimming method very carefully, in the order suggested here:

Read carefully the title and the introduction.

Next read the conclusion, which often summarizes the chapter, or at least gives the main points of the chapter.

Now go back and see how the writer reached the conclusion or developed the main idea. Be sure you understand each heading and subheading. Skim a paragraph or two in each section to be sure.

When you have finished going through the chapter by this method, make a final check. Look back quickly at the title, introduction, headings, and conclusion. Have you identified the main thought and development of the chapter? If so, you have accomplished your purpose.

STAGE I:
EMPHASIS ON ACQUIRING INFORMATION

TEXTBOOK PURPOSE AND METHOD

To understand a college textbook, you should first examine the author's purpose and method. Then examine the organization of the book.

The purpose in writing may be to <u>inform</u> or it may be to <u>influence</u> or <u>persuade</u>. Perhaps the purpose is to supply information, to give facts or other kinds of information, such as the sequence of military actions during the Civil War. Perhaps the writer is trying to persuade you of something. That the American Revolution was a mistake. That Lincoln was, after all, a scoundrel. Or that the American colonies were better off united and self-governing. That Lincoln was a man of conscience.

Maybe the writer is trying to help you <u>visualize something</u>, such as the relation of the sun to its various satellites, or the movement of iron filings toward a magnet. Or the author may be trying to help you <u>understand</u> a concept, an idea, such as torque; the how or why of an event; the different kinds of politicians, vegetables, or wars.

Now, how does a writer go about achieving a specific purpose? In other words, what is the writer's *method?*

Let us say we want to persuade you that the "good old days" were better than today. That would be our purpose—persuasion. The *method* might be to <u>tell a story or anecdote</u>; to <u>give reasons</u>, including cause and effect; to <u>give examples</u>, real or imaginary; to <u>quote</u> famous people, or our own Uncle George; to <u>analyze</u> the situation then and now; to <u>present facts and details</u>, carefully selected; or to <u>use slanted language</u> —nice words for the good old days, nasty ones for now.

Other methods that can be used on occasion are to <u>classify</u> things or people; to <u>describe</u> (give a word picture); to <u>compare</u> or <u>contrast</u> two or more points; and to <u>define</u> a term.

So the writer's method of achieving a purpose can vary. As you read a textbook, it will help if you understand the writer's purpose and method.

STUDY HINTS ON PARAGRAPH CONTENT

The paragraphs in your college textbooks give you a variety of information and ideas. Suppose, for example, you are reading about the development of the atomic bomb. That's your topic.

A paragraph under this general topic may tell you *who* helped develop the bomb—scientists in more than one country. You may be told *where* and *when* this happened. Or the paragraph may explain *why* the final decision was made to develop the bomb and use it during World War II, or *how* it operated, or *what* its ingredients were.

A questioning approach to a paragraph will help you to grasp the content more easily. *Who* or *what*? *When, where, why,* or *how*? As you read a paragraph, look in this questioning way for the kind of information given.

Try the questioning approach to this paragraph.

The Grand Canyon in northwest Arizona is a great tourist attraction. It was formed by the Colorado River as it cut through soil and rock during many long centuries, gradually creating the immense canyon we see today.

Does the paragraph tell us *who, what, when, where, why,* or *how*? More than one of these questions apply here. Which ones?

The paragraph tells us _____

Now try this paragraph.

The Grand Canyon in northwest Arizona is a great tourist attraction. From the great height of the canyon walls, visitors see a stunning view of the beautiful river below, looking like a silver thread. The walls themselves, with their layers of rock of various colors, are lovely to behold. For some visitors, the scientific aspect of these rocky layers is the main attraction.

The paragraph explains the same first sentence in a different way.

It tells us _____

Study Hints on Finding the Main Idea

Many of the paragraphs in your college reading contain what is called a topic sentence—a sentence stating the main idea of the paragraph. This may be the first sentence. But in some paragraphs the very first sentence is introductory, and the main idea is stated in the second sentence. In other paragraphs the topic, or main-idea, sentence may come in the middle or even at the very end.

EXERCISE 1   Identifying the Topic Sentence

Locate the topic sentence in this paragraph.

> The island of Great Britain includes England, Scotland, and Wales. Americans enjoy visiting this island for many reasons. There are great cities, neat country villages and fields, ancient houses, such natural wonders as the white chalk cliffs of Dover, and the colorful customs of English royalty.

The topic sentence in the paragraph comes _____

Try the next paragraph.

> The Great Dane makes a good pet. This large dog has an impressive and even distinguished appearance. It is also generally amiable and makes a dependable companion for its owner.

Here, the main idea is stated in sentence number _____

One more try.

> In this tiny mountain village, Peter finally found a good job. Soon he discovered that the townspeople were friendly. He came to love the mountain valley. The village became a real home to him.

In this paragraph the main idea comes _____

Our last paragraph does have a main idea, but there is no topic sentence stating it. As you read, look for the main idea of the paragraph as a whole.

> Benjamin Franklin showed his first talent as a young journalist writing for his brother's newspaper. Because of his diplomatic talents, he became an American representative first in England and later in France. His inventions won him international fame. A talent for wise and witty sayings made his *Poor Richard's Almanack* successful at home and abroad. Even as a conversationalist Franklin was talented.

The main idea of this paragraph is that _____

_____

WORLD HISTORY   Hiroshima

Our first paragraph is about an important event that took place in the Japanese seaport of Hiroshima. (The third syllable of the name is stressed and is pronounced like our word *she*—Hiro*shi*ma.)

> [1]It was fifteen minutes after eight on the morning of August 6, 1945. [2]The city was peaceful. [3]Suddenly a great flash of light cut across the sky. [4]Twenty miles away and more, people saw it and heard a tremendous explosion. [5]In that moment a hundred thousand people were killed. [6]Thousands more were blinded or crippled, or permanently weakened by the radiation sickness which this explosion caused. [7]Moreover, sixty-eight thousand buildings, many of them homes, were destroyed or damaged beyond repair. [8]The Japanese city of Hiroshima had been bombed by the United States, and the entire human race had entered a new era—the atomic age.

The bombing of Hiroshima was an important event during World War II. On the orders of President Harry S. Truman, the U.S. Air Force dropped the first atomic bomb on this Japanese city; the second was dropped on Nagasaki. Japan surrendered shortly thereafter.

EXERCISE 2   Answering Questions on "Hiroshima"

1. Read the first question, but before answering it go back to the paragraph itself. The paragraph about Hiroshima is mostly

   A. facts   B. opinion   C. argument   Which one? _____

2. The topic of our paragraph is clear. It's about the bombing of Hiroshima. But it may be a bit hard to decide on the main idea of the paragraph, the major point that the writer is making about the topic. Consider these three possibilities.
   A. The suddenness of the bombing, the size of the flash and explosion. The first two sentences of the paragraph are introductory. Next we have sentences dealing

      with the flash and explosion. These are numbers _____. There's no reason to choose this as the main idea. What follows is more important.
   B. The destruction of human life and property. Which sentences deal with this?

      Numbers _____. You might choose this as the main idea of the paragraph because of the space given to the point. It is important.
   C. The beginning of the atomic age for the entire human race. Which sentence

      deals with this? Number _____. You might also choose this as the

      main idea of the paragraph. Why? _____

      _____

Many paragraphs clearly have *one* main idea. Others may have two ideas that are important.

3. Look back at the second sentence: "The city was peaceful." This sentence could have been left out, because it's not really necessary. Why, probably, did the author include it?
   A. because it had always been a peaceful city
   B. for contrast with the violence that occurs
   C. because this was the city that was bombed   A, B, or C? _____

4. The paragraph deals with certain aspects of the bombing but not with others. Check (√) below the aspects that are covered.

   A. _____ time of bombing   D. _____ place of bombing

   B. _____ reason for bombing   E. _____ American reaction to it

   C. _____ results of bombing   F. _____ significance of it

5. The *tone of voice* a writer uses is often important to the reader. The tone of voice here is
   A. sentimental, almost tearful
   B. calm and factual, not excited
   C. tense and very angry   Which one? _____

6. In the final sentence, we have a dash (—) between "a new era" and "the atomic age." Look back at this sentence. The relationship between the two phrases is that
   A. the second merely *repeats* the first
   B. the second *contradicts* the first
   C. the second *explains* the first   Which one? _____

7. Sometimes, when we receive some information about an important event, we want to know more. If you were to read more about the bombing of Hiroshima, what

   would you like to know? _____

   _____

AMERICAN HISTORY   Washington and the Founding of the Nation

Note the five periods of time mentioned in the paragraph below: (1) the revolt of the American colonies against government by England; (2) the war itself; (3) the postwar period; (4) the Constitutional Convention; (5) the organizing of the new government.

> In his own time, Washington was called "the Father of His Country." It is hard to measure his importance in the founding of the new nation. He was just the kind of man the people of his generation admired most. Devoted to the revolutionary cause, he combined great strength of character, personal courage, and proven military ability. Because of these outstanding qualities, Washington became the leader the colonists rallied around in their revolt against English control. During the war with England, his influence increased. And after the English surrender, Washington's prestige was greater than that of Congress itself. He increased it by refusing the royal crown offered by those who wanted an American king. Later, after the peace treaty had been signed, he modestly resigned his post as commander-in-chief in order to become a private citizen. Next came the Constitutional Convention, which produced the Constitution that is still the basis of our government. Those who planned the Convention were careful to secure Washington's approval at the very beginning. They knew that his support was essential. Finally, Washington was called upon to take the lead, as first President of the United States, in organizing the new government.

Did you follow the five periods of time—rebellion, war, postwar, Constitution, new government? If not, read the paragraph again, and give it your full attention.

EXERCISE 3   Answering Questions on "Washington and the Founding of the Nation"

1. A. In this paragraph, the topic is clear. The paragraph is about a

_____

    B. The main idea—what is said about the topic—is sometimes harder to find. Look for the topic sentence, the sentence that gives you the main idea of the paragraph. The topic sentence, you remember, often comes first, almost as often second, and sometimes at the end.

    The main idea of the paragraph as a whole is
    (1) the idea in sentence 1 (Washington's title, "Father of His Country")
    (2) the idea in sentence 2 (his significance in the founding of the country)
    (3) the idea in the last sentence (his election as president)
                                    Which one? _____

2. The purpose of the paragraph, then, is to
    A. explain the process by which Americans awarded a title to Washington
    B. persuade us of Washington's military ability
    C. help us understand Washington's significance in the founding of the country

Which one? _____

Before you go on, check to see that your answer to this question agrees with your answer to question 1. After all, the main idea of a paragraph and its purpose should be pretty much the same.

3. The paragraph contains some analysis (of Washington's character), some persuasion (of his importance), and some historical facts (events, actions). The overall *organization* of the paragraph is
    A. a simple list of events of various kinds and times
    B. a time sequence; events in the order in which they happened
    C. an argument pro and con (for and against)   Which one? _____

4. When you take a test, you are often required mostly to give a *main idea* and the *main supporting details* from the passage or chapter you've studied.
    Suppose for a moment you are taking a quiz on a chapter that includes the paragraph on Washington. You are asked an essay-type question. You realize that a careful answer is important; a careless, sloppy answer will not count for much. Try to answer the question below in two or three careful sentences. Here's the question, the kind often called a *discussion question.*

    Discuss the significance of Washington in the founding of the nation.

    Begin by echoing the question. You could say something like "Washington was significant in the founding of the nation because . . ." Then you need supporting points. Remember the five time periods around which the paragraph is organized.

_____

_____

_____

_____

_____

_____

_____

_____

EDUCATION   The Montessori Method

Dr. Maria Montessori was an Italian educator who was active during the first half of the twentieth century. Today there are Montessori schools in a number of countries, including the United States. Most Montessori students are preschoolers, typically three or four years old.

In case you don't know the word *edict*, it suggests in this context a saying that has authority and is a kind of rule.

Children who enter a Montessori class for the first time begin work on a wide range of activities related to real life. They discover how to manipulate shoelaces, buckles, snaps and bows by practicing with these objects mounted on small wooden frames. They learn to serve juice, scrub their hands, clean their work area when they are finished, and move their chairs quietly when sitting or rising. These jobs are not intended solely to teach a youngster domestic chores. "Children experience joy at each fresh discovery," said Dr. Montessori. "Their satisfaction encourages them to seek new sensations and discoveries." Preparation for such tasks is in the spirit of Dr. Montessori's edict: "Teach the importance of doing even the smallest task well." Through expanding abilities gained in these early assignments, children begin to see order in apparent confusion. They begin to acquire the independence that comes with working for oneself. They begin to learn how to start and finish a job. Perhaps most important, they begin to understand what they can do.

EXERCISE 4   Answering Questions on "The Montessori Method"

1. The topic of the paragraph is the Montessori style of early education. The writer's purpose is to help us understand the Montessori approach. What would you say is the overall *method* of the paragraph?
   A. analysis (careful examination from several angles)
   B. narrative (story)
   C. slanted language   Which, A, B, or C? _____

2. The paragraph has three parts, containing these three elements: the *theory* behind this kind of schooling; the *activities* of the children; and the *results* in the children's development. Put these three elements in the order in which they appear in the paragraph: theory, activities, results.

   A. _____

   B. _____

   C. _____

   The paragraph has no obvious topic sentence stating the main idea. The closest we come is the last sentence. Read it over. This "most important" result is in a sense the main point of the paragraph.

From "Montessori Education Begins at Three" by Charles Mangel from *Look*, January 26, 1965. Reprinted by permission.

3. Writers often have a clear attitude toward a topic—that is, they approve in an obvious way or they clearly disapprove. But they might not state this attitude in so many words. We must read between the lines.

What seems to be the attitude of this writer toward the Montessori kind of early childhood education? On the whole, the writer's attitude seems to be
A. negative (disapproving)
B. positive (approving)
C. indifferent (having no particular attitude)   Which? _____

4. Toward the end of the paragraph the writer refers to "these early assignments." Writers often refer back to something they've told us earlier. In order to keep track of the line of thought in a passage, it's necessary to keep track of such references. Give two specific examples of early assignments mentioned in the paragraph.

A. _____

B. _____

5. As you understand the Montessori method of educating children, which of these three does it value most highly? Which is most important?
A. group interaction—working as a group
B. individual development of the children
C. learning to do domestic chores   Which one? _____

SOCIAL PSYCHOLOGY   Thomas Paine and the American Public

Thomas Paine was a social and political radical who was an important influence during the difficult days of the American Revolution. Paine was a radical in religion also. Like Franklin, Jefferson, and others of the Founding Fathers of our country, he was a believer in "natural religion." Here's what he believed:

> . . . men by nature experience awe, fear, and wonder, and have the feeling of a great creator, as they see the extent and power of the physical world: the mountain ranges, the vast prairies, the fearful deserts, the ocean, the mysterious heavens. These are natural religious feelings.

Such feelings the deists called "the religion of nature" or "the religion of reason." Here is a paragraph about Paine.

[1]Tom Paine's pamphlet *Common Sense*, written in 1776, was a great call to arms; it was immensely influential in preparing the American public for the fight for independence from England. [2]Later his *Crisis* papers were read around the campfires of the revolutionary army, on the orders of Washington, to keep up the spirits of the men in the darkest days of the war. [3]Paine was the pamphleteer of the revolution, praised by the leaders of the new nation, beloved by his countrymen. [4]But *The Age of Reason*, written in France, with its disapproval of church or institutionalized religion, and its praise of "natural religion," turned the American public against him. [5]Actually, like Franklin, Paine was a religious man who happened to believe in natural religion, not in the conventional religion of church or synagogue. [6]Yet years after his death, he was still regarded with horror. [7]Natural religion was considered to be the same as atheism. [8]This was hardly logical, since the clearly stated purpose of his book was to fight against atheism, which was growing in France. [9]He wanted to show that there was a real and valuable natural religion available to replace the older religion of the Bible, which many Frenchmen found they could no longer believe in. [10]He repeatedly stated his belief in "one god," the great creator. [11]When Paine expressed his belief in independence, going with the trend of the time, he was praised by the public; when he expressed his belief in natural religion, going against the common beliefs, he was damned.

EXERCISE 5   Answering Questions on "Thomas Paine and the American Public"

1. This paragraph contains some general points about the reaction of the American public to Paine and his work, as well as the reaction to three specific examples of his writing.
   A. First, let's take the general points. There is one sentence that sums up the attitude of the American public to Paine. This summary sentence is number

   (1) 1   (2) 2   (3) 11—the last sentence.   Which? _____

B. Now list the specific titles of Paine's political and religious works.

(1) political (revolutionary) _____

_____

(2) religious _____

2. Tom Paine wanted the colonists to fight for their independence from England. He probably called his revolutionary pamphlet (which urged the people to revolt) by the

title of *Common Sense* because it suggested that _____

_____

3. In answering an exam question, it's a good idea to use your own words as much as possible. This makes clear to your instructor that you understand what you're saying and haven't just memorized the material. In your words, finish this sentence:

Washington arranged to have Paine's *Crisis* papers distributed to his soldiers

during the war because _____

_____

4. In college, you are never asked merely to *read* something. Always, you are asked *questions* on what you have read. A discussion question demands an answer of at least one paragraph.

   In answering a question of this kind, your best method is to include the *general* point or points made in your reading, PLUS enough *specific* support to show your instructor that you have a solid knowledge of the subject. Be as brief as you can, but include the general point and also specific examples to answer this question.

What was the reaction of the American public to Paine and his works?

_____

_____

_____

_____

ZOOLOGY   The Honeybee

A rock painting in a Spanish cave, dating from prehistoric times, shows a man raiding a honeybee hive. The honeybee has been a friend to man for untold centuries. The honeybee we know, *Apis mellifica*, was introduced into New England early in the seventeenth century. Our familiar saying, "as busy as a bee," refers to this industrious creature. Central to the life of the honeybee hive is the queen, a bee that is fed on royal jelly by the worker bees and thus becomes a queen. The only function of the males (drones) is to provide many possible mates for the queen. Once mated, the queen can continue to lay fertile eggs for several years. At times she may lay a thousand or two a day, or even more. The busy worker bees, all female, must care for these eggs, and for the emerging young, as just one of their duties in helping to continue the honeybee species. The drones, who do no work, are tolerated until the supply of nectar decreases. Then these males are forcibly removed from the hive and are refused reentry by the guards at the entrance. A disabled worker will be removed just as promptly. Only productive workers are tolerated. Thus we see in the hive three castes: the queen, the productive worker bees, and the males, or drones. The bees that you and I commonly observe on a summer day in the country are all workers. We may see them on the alert, guarding the hive entrance, or flying about, busily gathering food for the hive. At the very height of its development, a hive may hold as many as 70,000 bees. New hives are created when the old queen leaves with a swarm and a new queen emerges. In her turn she will mate and begin to lay eggs. This process has continued for centuries.

EXERCISE 6   Answering Questions on "The Honeybee"

1. Which of the following is the *best* description of what we learn about the honeybee?
   A. the process by which the honeybees continue their species
   B. the role of the drones, or males
   C. the duties of the worker bees   Which one? _____

2. Instinctively the worker bees feed and care for the queen. This instinct of theirs is very important because
   A. they must have her to rule over the hive
   B. her eggs are needed for the continuation of the species
   C. the hive exists only for her   A, B, or C? _____

3. The workers remove some bees from the hive and let them starve. This is necessary to maintain the productivity of the hive. The two kinds of bees that are removed

   by force from the hive in this way are _____

   and _____

4. For centuries, people have studied, and wondered at, the organization and productive system of a honeybee hive. They have thought of ways in which it seemed to resemble human society. Think about this yourself.

Listed below are several ways in which a honeybee hive might be said to resemble human society. Some make sense and some don't. Check (√) the ways in which these bees seem to be like humans.

A. _____ provision for care of the young of the species

B. _____ for males, a mating role only

C. _____ concern for the survival of the species

D. _____ the discarding of disabled workers, leaving them to starve to death

E. _____ importance of gathering food

F. _____ a clear role or function for every individual—queen, workers, drones

G. _____ reproduction by only one female (the queen)

H. _____ the use of soldiers or guards

5. The queen bee actually has only one function or use—laying eggs. The drones also have only one simple but important function—mating with the queen. The workers, on the other hand, have several vital functions. On a zoology quiz, a typical question might be:

What are the duties of the honeybee workers?

In answering this question, what functions would you list? Five are given in the passage. How many duties of the workers do you recall?

A. _____

B. _____

C. _____

D. _____

E. _____

6. If you were to read more about honeybees and their life, what would you like to

read about? If nothing, just say so. _____

_____

_____

AMERICAN HISTORY   The Formation of Colonies

One method of exposition is *classification*—sorting people, or anything else, into kinds or classes. There are, as we all know, several kinds (or classes) of bus drivers: the nice, considerate ones; the cold but efficient ones; the unpleasant ones who seem to want to make us angry.

The paragraph below is devoted mainly to the classification of reasons why people leave home and settle in new colonies. Some notes on vocabulary follow the paragraph.

[1]Vermont was settled entirely from the other states of New England. [2]The inhabitants have, of course, the New England character, with no other difference beside what is accidental. [3]In the formation of colonies, those who are first inclined to emigrate are usually such as have met with difficulties at home. [4]These are commonly joined by persons, who, having large families and small farms, are induced for the sake of settling their children comfortably to seek for new and cheaper lands. [5]To both are always added the discontented, the enterprising, the ambitious, and the covetous. [6]Many of the first and some of all these classes are found in every new American colony during the first ten years after its settlement has commenced. [7]From this period on, kindred, friendship, and former neighbors prompt others to follow them. [8]Still others are allured by the prospect of gain, presented to the sagacious in every new country from the purchase and sale of lands; while not a small number are influenced by the brilliant stories which everywhere are told concerning most tracts during the early progress of their settlement.

covetous greedy	*sagacious* keen-witted; here, shrewd or clever in practical
induced persuaded	matters
kindred relatives	*tracts* specific areas of land

EXERCISE 7   Answering Questions on "The Formation of Colonies"

1. When reading a passage, in a textbook or elsewhere, the reader must be able to follow the writer's line of thought—the way one fact or idea follows another in a logical way. Sometimes the writer uses a *transition*. This is a word or phrase or sentence designed to move us smoothly from one point to another. For example, in switching from one period of time to another a writer may use a transition such as "ten years later" to keep us following the line of thought.

   The outline below shows the content of the Vermont paragraph in an orderly way. Note the transitional sentence between II, A, and II, B. Give the number of the sentence in which the writer makes each point.

   I. The settling of Vermont

   A. Settlers all from other New England states   _____

   B. All with the New England character   _____

   II. The settlement of colonies in general

   A. Reasons for settling in a new colony: the first ten years

   1. Difficulties at home   _____

   2. Large families, small farms   _____

   3. Discontent, enterprise, ambition, greed   _____

   Sentence 6 is a transitional sentence.

   B. Reasons for settling: after the first ten years

   1. Kindred, friends, former neighbors   _____

   2. Prospect of gain   _____

   3. Brilliant stories about the new colony   _____

   Go back and read through the outline. See how it shows clearly the development of ideas—the line of thought—in the paragraph.

2. How many sentences of the paragraph deal specifically with Vermont rather than with colonies in general?

   A. one   B. two   C. three   D. more than three   Which?_____

Take a moment to review the outline in question 1. See how the transitional sentence, number 6, fits into the plan of the paragraph.

MASTERING TERMINOLOGY
AND STUDYING ILLUSTRATED MATERIALS

Some study reading demands very careful study methods. Specialized reading demands special skills.

One skill is handling terminology—special words. As you read a passage in which terminology is important, study the specialized terms as you go along. Then review the passage and underline the important terms. Try to fix them in your mind. Remember, the best time for a first review is immediately after your first reading. If a term is really important—like *photosynthesis* in botany—you might try *over*learning. This is a learning method that involves repeated study until you respond automatically, without effort.

As an example of how to study terminology, let's look at a passage on organic compounds. The first section of the passage deals with carbohydrates. Here's a condensed version of the introduction and the basic information on carbohydrates. Note that the author has tried to help by tabulating the three kinds of carbohydrates.

ORGANIC COMPOUNDS

The principal organic compounds of living things include carbohydrates, lipids, proteins, and nucleic acids.

Carbohydrates. Some important carbohydrates are glucose, maltose, sucrose, and starch.

Monosaccharides: glucose, fructose, galactose

Disaccharides: maltose, sucrose (table sugar), lactose (milk sugar)

Polysaccharides: starch (storage form of sugar), cellulose, glycogen

We want to review this section on carbohydrates before going on to other kinds of organic compounds. We have been told in the introductory statement that four forms of carbohydrates are "important." So what we should do is go back and underline first the three subheadings and then these four important terms. Do this yourself for practice. Underline the three headings and the four terms, glucose, maltose, sucrose, and starch. Can you see how doing the underlining in itself helps fix the general scheme in your mind? The same process applies to studying not only somewhat technical material like this, but to textbook material in general.

A second special skill is making good use of charts, drawings, maps, or whatever illustrative help the author has provided. This skill involves relating the illustration to the text. Seldom does a drawing, for example, stand on its own. The writer gives you a background for it, then uses the drawing to make some basic information clearer to you. As you work with the illustrated material that follows, here and later in this book, you will acquire skill in relating illustrations to the explanations in the text.

Reading illustrated study material demands careful attention to relationships and to detail. This is true of all study reading, of course. But most students need an even more methodical, careful, and time-consuming method in order to master an illustrated textbook passage. Read once, then read again, for real mastery of this study material.

GEOGRAPHY   Time Zones

The United States is a big country, big enough to cover four time zones in the continental United States (not including Hawaii and Alaska). There is a one-hour difference between one time zone and the next.

Let's take a look at one American living on the Eastern Coast, in New York City. Let's call her Maria. She gets up at seven, has her breakfast, and goes off to work. At nine o'clock she's just starting her work for the day. Her brother Juan, who lives in Seattle, Washington, on the West Coast, is still sound asleep. His alarm clock is set for seven, but he still has another hour to sleep before it goes off, because it's only six o'clock in Seattle.

At night Maria walks into her apartment around six and puts on some comfortable clothes. As she settles down to eat her dinner, she turns on the 6:30 news. What's brother Juan doing? Still hard at work, he hasn't even begun to think about 5:00 P.M.—quitting time. In Seattle, it's only 3:30 in the afternoon.

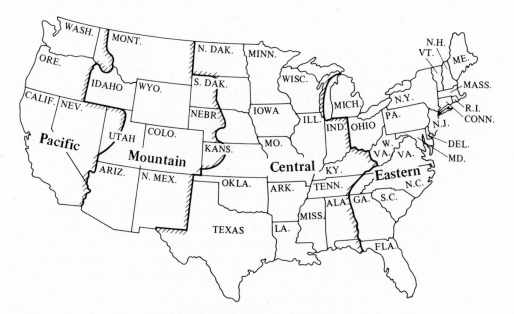

Time Zones in the Continental U.S.

"Jet lag" is a term invented to describe what happens to people who travel by air from one time zone to another. Adjusting to a new time schedule is confusing and tiring. Let's see what happens to another American, Alan Hanson, when he flies from Cleveland, Ohio, to Denver, Colorado, crossing two zone lines. As he reaches his hotel in Denver, he glances at his watch, which says six o'clock. He's had one drink on the plane. He is tired, hungry and ready for dinner. But the hotel clock says that it's only four. Dinner? "Sorry, sir, dinner service begins at six. Perhaps a sandwich in the coffee shop?"

Which time zone do you live in? What time is it for you when Maria turns on the 6:30 news in New York? When Alan Hanson arrives at his hotel in Denver?

EXERCISE 8 Answering Questions on "Time Zones"

1. A. The sun rises in the east, so as we travel westward across the time zones, is it

   earlier or *later* in the day? It's _____

   B. As we travel eastward, it's _____ in the day.

2. Which American state gets the first glimpse of sunlight, according to the map?

   The state of _____

3. The state of Nebraska is cut into two parts by a zone line. The eastern part of the state is in the Central Time Zone, while the western part is in the Mountain Zone. Bill Brown flies from his hometown in eastern Nebraska to a city in western Nebraska. His plane leaves at exactly 2:00 P.M. What time is it in the city where

   the plane lands exactly twenty minutes later? It's _____ P.M.

4. You live in the Eastern Time Zone. You want to phone your cousin in California the minute she gets home from work—about 5:30 P.M. Pacific Time. At what time

   should you call her? At _____ P.M.

5. Each zone has its *standard* time, for example, Central Standard Time. But time may vary within the zone. Let's go back to Nebraska. As we know, Omaha, to the east, is on Central Standard Time. Bridgeport, to the west, is on Mountain Standard Time. At noon in Omaha it will be 11:00 A.M. in Bridgeport. Now suppose that at this moment Omaha is on Daylight Saving Time. Sarah Brown must get up an hour earlier than she would by Central Standard Time, and her school opens an hour earlier.

   Suppose that it's midnight in Omaha by Sarah's clock. She's sound asleep, with her alarm set for six. Her cousin, Sue Brown, in Bridgeport, which is on Mountain Standard Time, is also asleep. Her alarm is set for six also.

   Whose alarm will go off first? Sarah's? Sue's? Or will they go off at the same

   time? _____

CONSERVATION   Forests and Deer in Pennsylvania

The forests of Pennsylvania were gradually harvested as the land was settled. The process accelerated. After 1890, extensive lumbering occurred—a very profitable operation. Fortunes were made in lumber. Fires increased under these conditions; in one year, a million acres of forest land burned in the state. Most of the present forests originated after such double destruction. The deer population, already declining sharply in numbers, was reduced still further as this destruction took place.

Also there were no restrictions on hunting, and tens of thousands of deer were shot by professional hunters, who lured the deer with salt licks and hunted them with dogs. Deer meat was sold very profitably in Pennsylvania markets, and the hunters grew rich. By 1900 deer were so scarce that the public became concerned.

The Pennsylvania Game Commission was created, and very shortly outlawed the use of dogs and salt licks in hunting. Also, about 1900, the Commission forbade hunting for the public market.

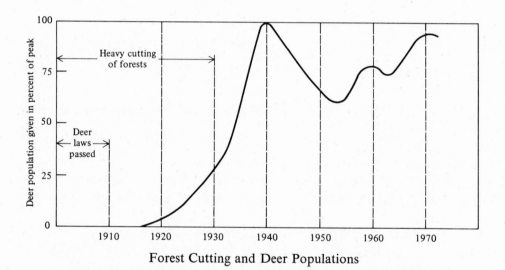

Forest Cutting and Deer Populations

From "Pennsylvania's Allegheny Hardwood Forests" by David A. Marquis. Used by permission of *Pennsylvania Forests*.

These legal measures, together with the plentiful food in the reviving forests, had such an effect on the deer population that by 1925 deer were numerous and became a problem. They were harming both farmers' crops and forest revival. Every woody plant less than six feet tall was destroyed in some areas. Then as food became scarce many deer died over the winter. This winter mortality, plus regular hunting seasons, gradually reduced the number of deer.

The management of forest resources and of the deer population has now become a matter of serious concern in Pennsylvania and is under continual study by various state agencies. Let us hope that the future will see a balance between the needs for forest renewal, the deer population, and the Pennsylvania hunting tradition, which goes back to the earliest days of the settling of the state. All three needs are very real; all must be considered.

EXERCISE 9 Answering Questions on "Forests and Deer in Pennsylvania"

1. The passage and chart on page 62 show us the relationships among three factors: heavy forest cutting, the deer population, and deer laws. The *overall* focus of the passage and chart is on
   A. deer laws
   B. heavy forest cutting
   C. the deer population   A, B, or C? _____

2. What two forces worked to reduce the number of deer in Pennsylvania before 1900?

   A. _____

   B. _____

3. The motive, or reason, for the extensive lumbering and the professional deer

   hunting was—look carefully— _____

4. What two factors helped to increase the deer population to damaging size?

   A. _____

   B. _____

5. Look at the chart and find how many years passed after the passage of the important deer laws (1910) before the deer population began to increase. This took

   about _____ years.

6. The damage done when deer were too numerous was of two kinds:

   A. damage to _____

   B. damage to _____

7. Consult the chart once more.

   A. After the peak of 1940, the lowest level of deer population was reached in the

      year _____, approximately.

   B. Judging by the chart, do you think the deer population in 1973 would have been thoroughly under control? As a guess, would you check yes or no?

      Yes _____   No _____

BIOLOGY   Evolution and the Embryo

Some terms are defined in the passage, others at the bottom of the page. Watch for the definitions within the passage itself.

The first forms of life appeared on earth about 2 billion years ago. Later came the first invertebrate life in the sea, then vertebrate life, then land animals, and, millions of years later, the early mammals. More modern mammals appeared some 25 million years ago. Early humans developed from these mammals. Then, perhaps about 50,000 years ago, modern man began to develop.

Perhaps the clearest demonstration of our ties to our animal ancestors is the development of the human embryo—the gradual formation of a human baby from a fertilized egg. Let's compare three stages in the development of a fish, a salamander, a tortoise, a rabbit, and a human being.

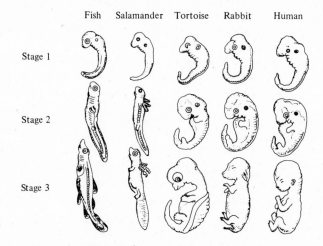

Development of the Embryo

Three points are worth noting. First, all the embryos appear quite similar in the first stage. The human, at the beginning, looks remarkably like the fish. To see the similarity, follow Stage 1 across the top of the illustration. The second point to notice is that all forms have a tail during development. In the human the tail disappears. Less clear from the drawing is the third point, the fact that at one stage all have gill slits. In fish, these contain gills for breathing. In land animals, they disappear.

Though the five animals are quite similar in Stage 1, they become very different in Stage 3. To see this, look across the bottom of the figure at Stage 3.

The study of embryology shows that all these animals are descended from a common ancestor. And as each individual embryo develops, it goes through the various stages in the evolution of its own species. Even in its final stages, it never loses some features of these earlier stages, such as the tailbone in humans. The fertilized human egg must repeat, in the womb, the various steps in the development of our species before it reaches the form we see as a newborn baby.

fertilized egg   the female egg made fertile by male sperm

invertebrate   having no spinal column

mammal   an animal that nurses its young

vertebrate   having a spinal column

womb   female organ within which the embryo develops

EXERCISE 10   Answering Questions on "Evolution and the Embryo"

1. Some words are defined in the passage, some in the glossary below it.

   A. For example, the word *vertebrate* means _____

   B. The word *mammal* means _____

   C. The word *embryo* means _____

2. Which of the three stages shown seems to correspond to the statement in the passage that "all these animals are descended from a common ancestor"? In which stage

   do they all look pretty much alike? This is Stage _____

3. Look at the first column of the illustration, the one labeled FISH. Follow the fish from Stage 1 through Stage 2 to Stage 3. Do the same for the salamander, tortoise, rabbit, and human. Note that some of the species go through fewer changes as they progress from Stage 1 to Stage 3. In other words, they don't develop as much.

   One of these species, as seems clear from the figure, is the _____

4. In the third stage, shown across the bottom of the figure, the rabbit and the human have forelegs or arms. These are also shown in another animal, the

   _____

5. During its development, the human embryo has two vestigial parts that disappear.

   These are the _____ and the _____

6. The rabbit and human embryos are somewhat similar in Stage 3. Legs (and arms in the human) are quite similar. Of course, the rabbit embryo shows a tail and the human embryo does not. Apart from the tail, the main difference in form between the two is a difference in the head. It's an important difference.
   Look carefully at the head of the Stage 3 rabbit embryo and the head of the Stage 3 human embryo. What's the difference?

   _____

   _____

   _____

   _____

   _____

BOTANY   A Green Leaf

Notice that in this passage **boldface** type has been used for important words. Many of these words are defined in the passage.

A green leaf manufactures food, the food on which we all depend for our very survival. The meat we eat comes from animals that eat grass and grain. Our fruits and vegetables are fed by their green leaves. A green leaf is like a factory that produces food.

Where does this factory get the energy that runs it? **Chlorophyll** is a green substance that allows plant cells to manufacture carbohydrates by using energy from sunlight. This process is called **photosynthesis**. *Photo* means light; *synthesis* here means the manufacturing process. All animal life depends on photosynthesis in green plants.

In a green leaf, the **palisade layer** is made up of cells that are rich in chlorophyll. Near the top of the leaf, they receive the sunlight. Here food is manufactured. To aid this process, water feeds up through the stem. The waxy **epidermis** (or skin), upper and lower, helps to prevent loss of water.

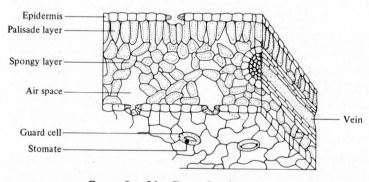

Green Leaf in Cross Section

Plants are essential for the survival of animals in a second way also. Plants use some of the carbon dioxide animals give off as they breathe, and the plants convert it into oxygen. The air we breathe would become poisonous without this exchange between plants and animals.

How does a green leaf make this exchange? The lower epidermis of each leaf contains **stomates**, openings that are opened or closed by their guard cells. Through them there is an exchange of carbon dioxide and oxygen, as they allow air to circulate through the air spaces within the leaf. Thus the leaf breathes.

As you look at a green leaf, remember the two ways in which such leaves make it possible for us to survive: (1) the manufacture of basic food, and (2) the exchange of carbon dioxide and oxygen, which keeps our air fit to breathe.

Name_____   Date_____

EXERCISE 11   Answering Questions on "A Green Leaf"

Many tests and quizzes use multiple-choice questions. This exercise is an example.

1. Field mice depend upon green plants; snakes eat mice; hawks eat snakes and mice. The food diagram below illustrates this.

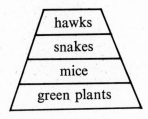

     The main point of the diagram is that:
     A. many animals eat one another
     B. hawks are superior to snakes and mice
     C. animal life depends on green plants   A, B, or C? _____

2. Photosynthesis would naturally be carried on
     A. both night and day
     B. mainly by night
     C. only by day   Which? _____

3. The leaf breathes through
     A. the guard cells
     B. the stomates
     C. the palisade layer   _____

4. One vital life cycle described in the passage is the exchange between green plants and animals of
     A. proteins, fats, and vitamins
     B. minerals and vitamins
     C. carbon dioxide and oxygen   _____

5. In the passage a number of terms are defined by the author. List four important terms that are defined for you.

     A. _____   C. _____

     B. _____   D. _____

READING TEXTBOOK SELECTIONS

The expert who wrote your textbook tried to explain the subject as clearly as possible. Most textbook writers make a real effort to organize their material in a simple and logical way, just as a highway planner tries to make it easy for you to drive on the highway by placing signs along the way to keep you posted.

Textbook writers use not only an introduction but headings and subheadings to help you follow the thought of a chapter. They also provide transitions—words or sentences, sometimes whole paragraphs—to aid you in going smoothly from one paragraph or section to the next. Often words or phrases that are very important appear in *italics* (slanting type) or in **boldface** (extra dark type) as a signal to you that these words need special attention.

To help you understand important points, an author supplies charts, photographs, or drawings. Your task is to relate these to the text. Try reciting—explaining in your own words the meaning of each chart or illustration. Summaries and study questions are additional aids and deserve close attention also.

Before beginning to study a chapter, preview it. Consider the title, read the introduction and headings, look for words in italics or boldface type, note the diagrams or pictures, and read the conclusion. Then settle down to study the chapter from beginning to end.

To open the very first chapter, a writer will probably discuss the subject of the book in a general way. The first textbook passage you will read in this section is the opening of a freshman text in astronomy. The author begins by telling you the subject matter of the science of astronomy—what astronomy is all about. This is one way of defining *astronomy*.

Naturally, your first task in studying any textbook is to understand thoroughly any definitions and general explanations the author gives you. These provide a basis for understanding the rest of the book.

At the beginning of each chapter, the writer usually tells you what the chapter will cover. It's very helpful to get this forecast clearly in mind before reading further. The introductory part of the chapter may be one paragraph or several. Only rarely will there be no introduction at all.

As you read each section of the chapter, relate the headings and any diagrams or pictures to the text. If there is a formula given, or a story told, ask yourself why. How is it related to the point of the section? As you read you may want to take notes, in a notebook or in the margin of the book. Or perhaps you will want to underline important words or sentences. But make sure you don't underline too much, because that can be very confusing.

To check your understanding of each section, review the material, or question yourself and recite. Remember that a single reading does not always produce real mastery of the material. Reread a section if you need to. Don't think this is a waste of time. It's not.

The best and easiest time to review an entire chapter is after you have finished going through it section by section. Never think you've completed your study of a textbook chapter unless you are clear—very clear—about the main points covered. Ask yourself, "Do I have a firm grasp of the main idea or ideas of the chapter? Do I have the significant details clearly in mind?" If you cannot state them in your own words, you must reread, restudy. You will read the next chapter more carefully!

When exam time comes, why do you sometimes find that you have forgotten so much, even though you have done your best to study well? As time passes and you study new material, you tend to forget what you have learned earlier.

What can be done to help you remember it?

One remedy is to keep in touch with your earlier learning. Look back at the first three chapters before you study the fourth. Skim through any class notes you have on the subjects covered in those three chapters. In other words, do some review in each course from time to time.

Perhaps you didn't learn your material thoroughly enough in the first place. Some students like to do what is often called *overlearning*. To overlearn, you must study, restudy, question yourself and recite, doing this over and over until you grasp the material so firmly that you know you won't forget. As a remedy for forgetting, this is an excellent system, but some review may still be necessary.

Serious and systematic study methods will help you master your college textbooks. There's no other way.

SCIENCE Astronomy

Do you remember the paragraph about Vermont that classified the reasons why settlers come to a new colony? This opening passage from *Astronomy*, a textbook by Robert H. Baker, begins by applying classification to the subject matter of astronomy, from small planets, like the earth, to huge star systems. The writer next classifies the reasons for studying astronomy in the past and in the present, and then introduces us to his subject, the vast physical universe in which we live.

<u>Imagination.</u>   Even when you are studying a scientific passage like this one, using your imagination will help you to grasp the material. Imagine yourself for the first time a student of the world of astronomy. Notice the pride of the writer as he argues for the high importance of his science—certainly one of the great sciences. And when he speaks of the Greeks six centuries before Christ (B.C.), imagine yourself living in that ancient world and believing firmly that the earth you live on is actually the motionless and stable center of the universe. You believe that it supports the sun, the other planets, the stars, the entire universe.

<u>Special terms.</u>   In this passage, the terms are mostly familiar: planets, stars, comets. *Interstellar* means between stars. Our author uses the word *system* to mean an immense group of stars. Our sun and earth lie within the system of the Milky Way, and the writer seems to assume that we are aware of this. You may already know the term "the Galaxy" for the Milky Way. But in this particular text, a star group of this kind will be called a *system*. When beginning a textbook, be sure you understand *the writer's terms*.

<u>Watching for synonyms.</u>   This textbook writer, like many others, sometimes changes his terms, uses synonyms, in order to avoid repetition. For example, when speaking of reasons or motives for the study of astronomy, he mentions as one reason "its usefulness" and "the ways in which the heavens have been useful to man." In the next paragraph he has different terms: "economic applications" and "survival and material welfare." But he means the same thing—usefulness.

Such use of synonyms or rephrasings is common in textbook writing. You must keep it in mind, and be on the lookout for synonyms or approximate synonyms.

<u>The writer's line of thought.</u>   As you read the textbook passage that follows, keep in mind also the importance of following the writer's line of thought. In the first section he speaks of the kinds of physical objects in the universe, the reasons for studying astronomy, and the purpose of the science. Then we have a <u>transition</u>. At the very end of the first section, he prepares us for a historical section by saying "as they have in the past."

At the very end of that section, he prepares us for his account of the modern view of the universe by saying "the more comprehensive view of the universe that we hold today."

Transitions such as these make it easy for us to follow the writer's line of thought.

INTRODUCTION TO ASTRONOMY

[1]*Astronomy*, the "science of the stars," is concerned not merely with the stars, but with all the celestial bodies which together comprise the known physical universe. It deals with planets and their satellites, including the earth, of course, with comets and meteors, with stars and the interstellar material, with star clusters, the system of the Milky Way, and the other systems which lie beyond the Milky Way.

[2]The most comprehensive of the sciences, astronomy is also regarded as the oldest of all. People of ancient times were attentive watchers of the skies. They were attracted by the splendor of the celestial scenery as we are today, and by its mystery which entered into their religions and mythologies. Astrology, the pseudo-science which held that the destinies of nations and individuals were revealed by the stars, furnished at times another motive for the study of the heavens.

[3]Still another incentive to the early cultivation of astronomy was its usefulness in relation to ordinary pursuits. The daily rotation of the heavens provided means of telling time. The cycle of the moon's phases and the westward march of the constellations with the changing seasons were convenient for calendar purposes. The pole of the heavens in the north, around which the Dippers wheel and having its place now marked roughly by the star at the end of the Little Dipper's handle, served as a guide to the traveler on land and sea. These are some of the ways in which the heavens have been useful to man from the earliest times to the present.

[4]But the value of astronomy must not be measured in terms of economic applications. Astronomy is concerned primarily with an aspiration of mankind, which is fully as impelling as the quest for survival and material welfare, namely, the desire to know about the universe around us and our relation to it. The importance of this service is clearly demonstrated by the widespread public interest in astronomy, and by the generous financial support which has promoted the construction and effective operation of great telescopes in rapidly increasing numbers. Nowhere in the college curricula can the value of learning for its own sake be more convincingly presented than in the introductory courses in astronomy.

[5]It is the purpose of astronomy to furnish a description of the physical universe, in which the characteristics and relationships of its various parts are clearly shown. At present, the picture is incomplete. Doubtless it will remain incomplete always, subject to improvements in the light of new explorations and viewpoints. The advancing years will bring additional grandeur and significance to our view of the universe, as they have in the past.

The Sphere of the Stars

[6]As early as the 6th century B.C., Greek philosophers regarded the earth as a globe standing motionless in the center of the universe. The boundary of the universe was a spherical shell, having the stars set on its inner surface. This *celestial sphere* was supported by an inclined axis through the earth, on which the sphere rotated daily, causing the stars to rise and set. Within the sphere of the

From the Introduction to *Astronomy* by Robert H. Baker. Reprinted by permission of Van Nostrand Reinhold Company.

stars seven celestial bodies moved around the earth; they were the sun, the moon, and the five bright planets.

[7]For more than two thousand years thereafter, this view of the universe, the universe of appearances, remained practically unchanged. The chief problem of astronomy was to account for the motions of the seven wandering bodies, so that their places in the heavens could be predicted for the future. The outstanding solution of the problem, on the basis of the central, motionless earth, was the Ptolemaic system.

[8]Copernicus, in the 16th century, proposed the theory that the planets revolve around the sun rather than the earth, and that the earth is simply one of the planets. The rising and the setting of the stars were now ascribed to the daily rotation of the earth. The new theory placed the sun and its family of planets sharply apart from the stars. With its gradual acceptance, the stars came to be regarded as remote suns, at different distances from us and in motion in different directions. The ancient sphere of the stars remained only as a convention; and the way was prepared for explorations into the star fields, which have led to the more comprehensive view of the universe that we hold today.

The Solar System

[9]The earth is one of a number of relatively small planets which revolve around the sun, accompanied by smaller bodies, the satellites, of which the moon is an example. They are dark bodies, shining only as they reflect the sunlight. The nine principal planets, including the earth, are somewhat flattened globes at average distances from the sun which range from four tenths to forty times the earth's distance. Thousands of smaller planets, the asteroids, describe their orbits in the middle distances. Comets and meteor swarms also revolve around the sun. Their orbits are, in general, more elongated than those of the planets, and they extend to greater distances from the sun.

[10]These bodies together comprise the solar system, the only known system of this kind, although others may well exist. A similar planetary system surrounding the very nearest star could not be discerned with the largest telescope. Likewise, the telescopic view of our system from the nearest star would show only the sun, now having the appearance of a bright star.

The Stars

[11]The sun is one of the multitude of stars, representing an average of the general run of stars. It is a globe of intensely hot gas 864,000 miles in diameter, and a third of a million times as massive as the earth. Some stars are much larger than the sun; others smaller, and a few scarcely exceed the planets in size. Blue stars have higher surface temperatures than that of the sun, which is a yellow star. The red stars are cooler; but all are exceedingly hot, as compared with ordinary standards.

Generalized Review of "Introduction to Astronomy"

All the sciences have value of some kind. Often they are very practical and helpful. But the practical uses of astronomy are not as important as the fact that this science satisfies our desire to understand the place of humans in the universe.

The earth is not the center of the universe, as people believed for thousands of years, but is just one planet revolving around an average star, the sun, which is one of millions of stars in the huge star system of the Milky Way. Beyond the Milky Way lie many other star systems, which we may know more about in future years.

A Question for Thought or Discussion

The Greeks viewed the universe as relatively small—a neat sphere containing moon, planets, stars—with the earth as the center of it all. And humans were the lords of the earth.

Now we know that we live on a small planet circling around an average star, an insignificant part of one star system, the Milky Way. There are many star systems. Our earth is a tiny speck in a vast universe.

Human beings seemed important to the ancients in their earth-centered universe. A Greek philosopher once said, "Man is the measure of all things." The question is: could we say that today?

Your Exercise on the Passage

As you work on the following exercise, refer back freely to the astronomy passage. This is not a memory exercise. It is a *reading-thinking* exercise. Don't hurry, but work at a speed that is comfortable for you.

EXERCISE 12   Answering Questions on "Introduction to Astronomy"

1. In the second sentence of the first paragraph, the author lists the celestial bodies that make up the known physical universe. The *order* of the list is important. It goes from smaller bodies (planets, like the earth) to larger and largest (star systems).

   Notice that there are four groups of bodies, each group being introduced by the preposition *with*. The author thus classifies the heavenly bodies into four groups. Using *with* as your guide, carefully list, in order, these four classifications.

   Group 1: with _____

   Group 2: with _____

   Group 3: with _____

   Group 4: with _____

   It is easier to remember four clear-cut classifications than ten separate items.

2. The sentence you were working with above was a list. As you read, it is important for you to follow the organization and thought of each sentence. Check your understanding of the three sentences that follow.
   A. *Paragraph 2, sentence 1.* Here the author tells us two qualities of astronomy, both given as superlatives. What's a superlative? Words and phrases like *most reliable* and *hottest* are superlatives—they compare more than two things or people.

      The two superlative qualities of astronomy are expressed in the phrase

      _____ and the word _____

   B. *Paragraph 3, sentence 4.* The subject of this sentence is "the pole of the heavens in the north." But the *subject* is separated from the *verb* by a long interrupter set off with commas. The verb comes near the end of the sentence— "*served* as a guide to the traveler." Review the sentence; see the commas that set off the interrupter. The question is, *what* served as a guide to the traveler?

      _____

   C. *Paragraph 4, sentence 2.* Again we have an interrupter between two related parts—this time between two nouns. The first of these is the noun "aspiration," in the phrase "an aspiration of mankind." Later in the sentence another noun phrase explains to us what this aspiration is. What *is* this aspiration of mankind?

      _____

3. Do you know what a value judgment is? The writer of this passage makes a value judgment. That is, he says that one thing has more *value* than another—it is more worthwhile. Paragraph 4 opens: "But the *value* of astronomy . . ."

   A. On what reason for studying astronomy does the writer set a high value? What important desire of human beings does this study satisfy? (Use your own

   words.) _____

   _____

   _____

   B. What reason for studying astronomy seems to the writer to be *less* valuable?

   _____

   _____

4. *Outlining.* The passage has four sections. Choose one of the headings listed here for the first five paragraphs, and write it in beside I. Choose another for paragraphs six, seven, and eight (II). Here are some possible headings.

   The Study of Astrology   Two descriptions of the Universe: Greek and
   Planets and Their Place   Copernican
        in the System   The Study of Astronomy

   I. (Paragraphs 1–5) _____

   II. (Paragraphs 6–8) _____
   III. The Solar System
   IV. The Stars

5. On the question whether there are other solar systems like ours (sun, earth, other planets), the writer comments that "others may well exist." The closest rephrasing of this would be
   A. it is *quite unlikely* that other solar systems exist
   B. it is *very likely* that other such systems exist
   C. it is *possible* that other such systems exist   Which one? _____

6. *Time* references are important. At the end of paragraph 8, the author speaks of "the more comprehensive view of the universe that we hold today." He is referring in a general way to
   A. the date when you are reading this exercise
   B. the date when Copernicus proposed his theory
   C. the date when this textbook on astronomy was written   Which? _____

7. *Visualizing*, that is, getting a mental picture of what the author is describing, can be helpful or even necessary. Paragraphs 6 and 7 describe the universe as the Greeks saw it. It is really necessary to visualize, to get a mental picture, in order to understand this description.

   Draw a simple diagram of the earth and heavens as the Greeks saw them and *label the parts*. This will show the way people viewed the universe for more than 2,000 years.

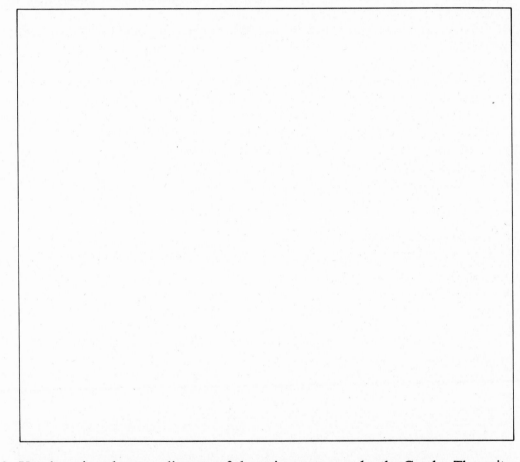

8. You have just drawn a diagram of the universe as seen by the Greeks. The writer calls this "the universe of appearances," in contrast to the universe as we understand it today. Why? Choose *two answers* from those given below. All the statements are correct, but only two explain *why*.
   A. The Greeks had to judge the universe by what they could *see*.
   B. The vast size of the universe is hard for the mind to grasp.
   C. Ptolemy, a Greek astronomer, best systematized the Greek view.
   D. Today we have telescopes that go beyond appearances and let us understand things we cannot see with the naked eye.

Two of these statements explain the writer's point. Give the letters of these two.

_____

9. We noted that the phrase "in the past," at the end of paragraph 5, is a transition that leads us into the next section, which deals with the past. And that "the more comprehensive view of the universe that we hold today" is a transition that leads us into the following section, which tells us how we view the universe today.

At the end of paragraph 10, there is a transition leading into the final section. Copy below the part of the last sentence of this paragraph that is a transition. Don't copy the whole sentence. Check carefully. What's the next section about?

Now write in the transition. _____

_____

10. EXTRA CREDIT QUESTION. You need not answer unless you want to try for extra credit.

A recent writer, speaking of drama (plays) today, remarked that most modern drama does not set a high value on human character and personality. Writers of plays nowadays do not seem to think of the individual as being very worthwhile. The writer believes that this attitude is the result of a "realization" of our "situation" in the universe, that is, a realization of our place on a tiny planet in the midst of a vast universe.

What part of the passage on astronomy would be related to, would help to explain, this comment?
A. the discussion of astrology as opposed to astronomy
B. the statements concerning the size and heat of the sun
C. the account of the change from the old earth-centered system to the Copernican system

Which one? _____

SOCIOLOGY   Groups and Grouping

Before going on to study our next selection, from *Sociology*, by John F. Cuber, a freshman text, we'll first turn to a generalized overview of it. The chapter we'll be reading from has the title "Groups and Grouping."

Generalized Overview of " Groups and Grouping"

Like other sciences, sociology has its own terms, or special names for things. These are often concept or idea words. For example, in sociology a *group* is any two or more people who communicate with each other, while a *category* is one kind of people (geniuses, say), who aren't ordinarily in touch with each other. People sitting silent on a bus are an example of an *aggregation*—they're physically together but are not communicating.

Why do we live with other people? Well, it's *not* because we are born with a need for group activity. Instead, our writer tells us, it is because we depend on others for things we have learned to want, whether airplane rides or refrigerators. So we live in groups. Some of our groups depend on common interests we have with certain other people. But we can also have very unfriendly relationships, so we need laws and courts to control our unfriendly behavior toward those we are in conflict with. On the other hand, we depend on certain special people to fix our teeth or sell us food, and these people depend on us for their livelihood. In this case we are interdependent—we depend on each other.

Introducing " Groups and Grouping "

Definitions are important in college textbooks. The author of this sociology text begins with a long paragraph defining the most important term in sociology: *group*. He calls this "the pivotal concept," the central idea, of sociology. The word has a special meaning in the technical nomenclature (terminology) of sociology.

In defining this and other terms, the author uses such words as *reciprocal* (two-way, back and forth), *interaction* (action back and forth), and *interdependence* (dependence on each other).

These three words, *reciprocal*, *interaction*, and *interdependence*, are used to express communication or dependence two-way, back and forth, between people.

Watching for synonyms and alternatives. The word *or* can be tricky. If we say " *He's either dumb or playing dumb*," we mean he's one or the other, not both. These are choices, alternatives. But if we say "*Tom Paine believed in deism, or natural religion*," then "natural religion" is both a synonym and a definition of deism.

The writer of the passage uses *or* between alternatives and also between synonyms. Keep this in mind as you read the text.

Organization, line of thought. This sociology passage has two parts. The first gives us definitions of three terms: *group, category, aggregation*. The second explains why people live in groups and the *kinds* of groups they live in (classification again).

Follow your author as he goes from one definition to another, then to the reasons for and the kinds of groups.

Imagination. How can imagination help you to understand definitions and classification? Try this. As you read the definition of *group*, for example, imagine yourself in communication reciprocally (back and forth) with one or more of your friends. You're talking to each other; you're a group.

Or, for *category*, think of yourself as one member of a large category: American college students. College students are one special kind of American. They make up one category.

For *aggregation*, imagine yourself on a jet plane crossing the Atlantic Ocean with a lot of other people, who don't know one another and don't communicate. (Start a conversation and what happens? You're part of a group.)

Imagination, which helps you to understand definitions, can also help you to understand the different *kinds* of groups in which people live and *why* they live in groups in the first place.

Try to use your imagination—participate in what you are reading. If you really participate, what you read will not be hard to remember. It will be hard to forget.

GROUPS AND GROUPING

[1]The term <u>group</u> is the pivotal concept of sociology. Since the word is loosely and variously used in popular language and in the language of other sciences, it is necessary to define somewhat precisely what it means in the technical nomenclature of sociology. Stated tersely, *a group is any number of human beings in reciprocal communication.* It may be well to emphasize certain aspects and implications of this short definition which beginning students, as well as some sociologists themselves, frequently overlook or do not appreciate fully. First, a group refers only to persons *in communication.* Mere physical closeness, if there is no communication, does not make a group. The communication creates the group, not the mere fact of spatial proximity or physical contact. Second, a group may be of any size from two persons to, theoretically and potentially, the entire population of the world. Third, communication need not be face-to-face or by "word of mouth," it may be indirect through writing or at long range through such instruments as the telegraph. Persons need not "know each other personally" in order to be in communication; they merely need to contact one another via language, oral or written or gestural. Finally, the persons in a group influence each other reciprocally; one-way communication does not form a group. This, of course, does not mean that the various persons in a group influence each other equally.

" Group" Distinguished from Other Human " Plurals"

[2]The concept of <u>the group</u> we are employing will perhaps become more clear when we have distinguished two other kinds of human pluralities—aggregations and categories.

[3]<u>The category.</u> A category is a number of persons who are *thought of* together, whether they are in communication or not. Morons are a category. So also are the males 40 to 44 years of age in the population of the United States, or all the women in the United States who have failed in college. None of these are groups, as we have defined the term, because *they are not ordinarily in intercommunication.*

[4]<u>The aggregation.</u> An aggregation is a collectivity of persons who are held together in a physical sense by some factor other than intercommunication. The populations of a country or of the world are cases in point. Aggregations may, of course, be groups also, but all aggregations are not groups because the people involved may not be in interaction.

Why Grouping?

[5]Wherever humans are found, they are living in groups. The universality of human grouping has attracted attention, and several false notions have arisen claiming to explain the "reason" for groups. These errors have become so widely diffused that it seems necessary to examine them critically at the outset.

Instinct or Learning?

[6]Perhaps the chief fallacy is the widespread explanation of human groupings in terms of an *inherited* "need" or "urge" or "instinct" for group activity.

From John F. Cuber, *Sociology: A Synopsis of Principles,* 3rd ed., © 1955, pp. 307–310. Reprinted by permission of Prentice-Hall, Inc., Englewood Cliffs, N.J.

Evidence for this explanation is lacking. Stated tersely, modern sociology finds that grouping is practically a necessity for most people—a necessity because through their socialization they have acquired, that is, learned, wants which can be satisfied effectively only by group participation. Each person has become so dependent in so many different ways upon other people that permanent and consistent living outside of groups is virtually unthinkable and impossible. From the birth cry to his burial, the desires of the human being are ministered to by other humans. While at times interaction with other people may not be wholly pleasant, the overall experience of his life is characterized by association with other people. Having learned, as everyone has, that he needs other people in order to satisfy his wants, there is no alternative. Group living becomes a necessity.

"Common Interest" or Functional Interdependence

[7]A second popular fallacy pertaining to groups is "common interest" . . . Men are said to be found everywhere functioning in groups because they have common interest, and through group participation the common interests are satisfied. Undeniably *some* of man's interests are common, but others are individualized or specialized, while some are openly antagonistic. Observe, for example, the larger number of groups found in the modern community which grow out of men's conflicts with one another. Courts, strike mediation boards, and legislative bodies are only a few of the many groups which come into existence because of conflicts among men. Other groups are made possible only by the fact of divergent, but not necessarily antagonistic, interests. The market-place, stores, banks, and schools come into being because different members of the society have different needs which can often be satisfied through interaction among persons, whose interests are reciprocal. Thus, the seller and the buyer form a brief group which fulfills the needs of the seller to sell and the buyer to buy. The bank provides a medium through which people who have money to lend for interest may make contact with persons having a desire to borrow money and are willing to pay interest for the privilege. Schools arise because there is a category and perhaps also a group of people (teachers) who have talents which they are willing to sell and which the pupils directly or indirectly buy. The teachers' interests are to sell their services and the students' to buy them. Thus it is readily demonstrated that the common generalization to the effect that groups are based on common interest is an oversimplification, or an exaggeration, of one factor which accounts only for the existence of *some* groups. A great many groups, possibly a majority, are based on divergent interests or antagonistic ones. All the evidence taken together would seem to indicate that groups are a practical manifestation of our interdependency upon one another.

Groups: *A Question for Thought or Discussion*

When we think of our friends and acquaintances, we realize that each one has a very separate and distinct personality. So do you and I.

What makes up a personality? It has been suggested that an individual's personality consists of a collection of roles that person plays. Carl, for example, within the family group plays the role of son and brother; he is also, outside the family, a neighbor, a college student, a member of a basketball team, a close friend of Greg and Bill—and in each of these family, school, and social groups he plays a different role. He may excel in one group, while being a poor performer in other groups. A good student may be a social failure.

Think of human personality—yours, say—as a collection of roles that you play in different groups. Is this a good explanation of what personality is? What do you think?

EXERCISE 13   Answering Questions on "Groups and Grouping"

1. A short and common word like *the* or *a* before a noun can be decisive in the meaning of a sentence. If you say "He's *the* winner in the contest" and if you say "He's *a* winner in the contest," you mean two different things. Which one means that there's only one winner? "He's *the* winner" does.

    The author's opening statement is: "The term *group* is the pivotal concept of sociology." When he says "*the* pivotal concept," he means
    A. there is only one pivotal concept in sociology
    B. there are two or more pivotal concepts in sociology
    C. there may be one or several pivotal concepts   Which one? _____

2. The first four paragraphs of this passage contain definitions of three terms: *group, category, aggregation*. As we have noted earlier, definitions are important in textbooks. They often appear at the beginning of a book or the beginning of a chapter. We must master them before going on.

    In order to show your mastery of the definitions given in the passage, mark each of the items in the list below with the letters that show which definition fits it best.

    GR for group   CA for category   AG for aggregation

    A. The members of the national Sierra Club   _____

    B. The members arguing at a local meeting   _____

    C. The voters of the United States   _____

    D. All the people in Chicago on a certain date   _____

    E. The legal residents of Chicago   _____

    F. Geniuses   _____

    G. The people traveling on a bus at the same moment   _____

    H. Atlanta bus drivers   _____

    I. A teacher and students having a discussion   _____

    J. Men and women in the armed forces in World War II   _____

    This is an important question. Check your answers before going on.

3. Obviously, the word *group* is important in this sociology text. A key word or phrase

in the author's definition of *group* is _____

Be sure that the word or phrase you have chosen helps to tell us an important quality of a group—something that makes it a group.

4. *Organization* is also important in understanding this selection.
   A. On the first page of the selection, paragraph 1 defines *group*. Paragraph 2 is a paragraph of introduction. It introduces
      (1) the rest of the chapter
      (2) the third paragraph only
      (3) the third and fourth paragraphs   Which? _____

   B. In the second part of this selection we have three headings. The first one, "Why Grouping?," is centered—that is, it appears in the center of the page. The other two are not. *Reread* the short paragraph under "Why Grouping?" first. Now decide why it is centered and the others are not.
      (1) "Why Grouping?" is more important than the other two.
      (2) "Why Grouping?" is less important than the other two.
      (3) "Why Grouping?" is not really related to what follows.   Which? _____

5. The word *or* is sometimes used to connect words that are synonyms—words that have the same general meaning. "Human groupings or plurals" is an example. At other times the word *or* connects words that are alternatives; you choose one or the other. "Friends or enemies" is an example of this.
   A. In the heading "Instinct or Learning?" the two terms "instinct" and "learning" are
      (1) synonyms—words having the same general meaning
      (2) alternatives, choices—one or the other, not both
      (3) neither of these   _____

   B. In paragraph 6, sentence 1, the words "need," "urge," and "instinct" are
      (1) synonyms—words having the same general meaning
      (2) alternatives, choices—one or the other, not both
      (3) neither of these   _____

   C. Now look at the next heading. Here the terms "common interest" and "functional interdependence" are
      (1) synonyms—words having the same general meaning
      (2) alternatives, choices—one or the other, not both
      (3) neither of these   _____

6. Paragraph 6 contains, first, an account of the "chief fallacy," or false idea, that people have about human groups. The paragraph then tells us what the writer believes is the truth about groups.

   A. The chief fallacy, or false idea, is _____

   _____

   B. The truth is _____

   _____

7. Give ONE example *of your own* of each kind of group listed below.

   A. Common interest _____

   _____

   B. Antagonistic interests _____

   _____

   C. Reciprocal interests, interdependence _____

   _____

READING POWER
FOR COLLEGE TEXTBOOKS

STAGE II:
INFORMATION AND INTERPRETATION

STAGE III:
ADVANCED READING POWER

STAGE II:
INFORMATION AND INTERPRETATION

LAW   The Dual Role of the Constitution

Most of us should know more than we do about the American Constitution. But we all feel that it is basic to our way of life.

Change the Constitution? Many Americans would be disturbed by the thought. Yet the Constitution has been amended many times and is stronger because of these amendments. The basic strengths of this document have never been challenged: its guarantees of freedom of speech, of religion, of the essentials of justice, and of the basics of democracy. In this sense, the Constitution remains unchanging. But in another sense, it must change and has done so. It grew as the nation grew from a mainly rural country of thirteen colonies to a vast industrial power with millions of citizens. New problems demand new answers. "The Constitution," declared Jefferson, "belongs to the living, not the dead." Each generation has had its role in the development and growth of the original instrument. Yet it still serves the original purposes: to establish justice, secure the blessings of liberty to ourselves and our posterity, insure domestic tranquillity, and provide for the common defense. Civil war, major economic depressions, the stresses of world wars, racial turmoil, political scandals—all these have come and gone. The Constitution continues as a protector of liberties and of our governmental system which, despite its problems, has given us, as a nation, a measure of stability. It serves the living, not the dead, because of its continuing adaptation to new conditions. The American Constitution plays a dual role, basically the same, yet ever changing.

**EXERCISE 14   Answering Questions on
"The Dual Role of the Constitution"**

1. Look for a topic sentence in the paragraph on the Constitution. Is there one? If so,

   which sentence? _____

   _____

2. The fourth sentence of the passage mentions four basic strengths of the American
   Constitution—four essential guarantees. These are guarantees of

   A. _____

   B. _____

   C. _____

   D. _____

3. Political scandals are mentioned, as well as depressions, wars, racial problems.
   What is the main point the passage makes about these events?

   _____

   _____

4. The Constitution is the basis of our system of government. We are told that despite
   stresses, depressions, and scandals, we have had "*as a nation, a measure of stability.*"
   This is not a really strong statement about stability. But it's an important point.
   Restate this idea *in your own words*, as well as you can.

   _____

   _____

5. The main point of the passage is the dual role of the Constitution. The Constitution

   is "basically the same" in one role, which is _____

   _____

   It is "ever changing" in the other role, which is _____

   _____

6. If the basic guarantees of the Constitution were removed, what do you think might
   happen?

   _____

   _____

   _____

BLACK STUDIES   Marcus Garvey

What was the Black Star Line? This steamship company was the creation of a gifted Jamaican who had come to the United States in 1916—Marcus Garvey. The Black Star Line was designed for trade between the United States and Africa. A further creation of Garvey's was the Negro Factories Corporation. Both of these creations were designed to strengthen the economic position of American blacks. Black manufacturing and black trade were his aims— economic muscle. His Universal Negro Improvement Association claimed at one time two million members, and by 1919 had branches in various cities. Through *The Negro World*, his newspaper, Garvey spoke to a growing audience, sending his message of brotherhood, improvement, and economic strength. He also stressed kinship and trade with African blacks. Garvey's dream ended in 1925, when legal and financial problems led to a jail sentence. Released from prison, he was deported to his native Jamaica, where he became a member of the municipal council of Kingston. Return to the United States, however, was barred. He died in London in 1940, but his message of racial common cause and economic enterprise was never lost. The name Marcus Garvey becomes increasingly important in the history of blacks in the United States.

EXERCISE 15   Answering Questions on "Marcus Garvey"

1. The above paragraph about Marcus Garvey, taken as a whole, is mostly
   A. argument
   B. persuasion
   C. facts   Which, A, B, or C? ———

2. Garvey believed that the path of advancement for American blacks was mainly
   A. religious faith
   B. economic strength
   C. racial pride   Which? ———

3. Writers sometimes make clear their attitudes toward someone they're dealing with. They may say, "He was an unfortunate influence," or perhaps, "He was a great and good man." This writer, however, tells us only that Garvey is important. We must try to read between the lines and figure out for ourselves whether there is any special attitude toward Garvey.

   The writer's attitude seems to be
   A. positive (generally in favor of Garvey)
   B. negative (generally against Garvey)
   C. neutral (neither for nor against to any degree)   Which one? ———

4. The paragraph is an account of Garvey's remarkable efforts. It is not a character sketch, nor a personal account of Garvey as a man. Still, we do learn certain things about Garvey. We learn them by reading about what he did and what his aims were. Considering the society of his time particularly, he accomplished a great deal.

Which of the qualities listed below do you think were characteristic of him? Check (√) the ones that seem to fit.

_____ selfishness   _____ good financial judgment

_____ unselfishness   _____ hopeful attitude

_____ strong personality   _____ pessimistic attitude

_____ ability to organize   _____ ability to persuade people

5. We are told that his aims were black manufacturing and black trade—"economic muscle." This is a figure of speech. "Muscle" here means
   A. hope
   B. power
   C. faith   Which one? _____

6. For every one of Marcus Garvey's aims, he had a specific organization. Beside each aim listed below, write in the name of the organization that was designed to further this aim.

   Aim   *Organization*

   A. black manufacturing   _____

   B. general improvement of blacks   _____

   C. getting his message to blacks   _____

   D. black trade   _____

7. Marcus Garvey in 1925 was legally convicted on genuine charges—selling stock through the mails when his Black Star Line was going bankrupt. He served his sentence and then was deported.
   At that time, aliens who got into trouble with the law were likely to be deported. Perhaps his troubles with the law were the only reason he was deported. They were sufficient. If, however, there was another reason why he might have been deported, what do you think it could have been? If you don't have any idea, just say so.

   _____

   _____

   _____

PSYCHOLOGY   Stress

¹We are all under stress, and from a fairly early age. ²Children are afraid of the dark, of unfriendly dogs, of losing their parents' love, of the neighborhood bully; and many adults have similar fears. ³In addition to fear, another kind of stress is anxiety. ⁴Students are anxious about their grades and their dates and their future plans; parents feel anxiety about their children's health and success in life. ⁵Both the young folks and the adults may feel another kind of anxiety, a feeling of inadequacy, perhaps about their intelligence or their ability to handle their life situations. ⁶Many everyday occurrences cause passing stress—events like driving in bad traffic, a sudden storm, a quarrel, a frown from the boss, a feeling of anger or guilt. ⁷More serious matters, such as a death in the family, a divorce, a serious health problem, loss of hard-earned property, cause deeper and longer-lasting stress. ⁸Other serious events, such as marriage, getting a great new job, sudden wealth, a joyous reunion with a loved one, can be stressful too. ⁹Yes, we are all under stress. ¹⁰Yet most of us manage to keep our cool to quite an extent, and keep going in spite of the stresses of our daily lives.

Notice that although many examples of stress are given, these examples tend to fall into general classes. Fear is one general *kind* of stress, and *examples* are given of this kind of stress. Children's fear of the dark is one example. But here even the examples are a bit on the general side; we read about children's fears, not about little Jimmy Braun's fears. *Children* is a general term, whereas *Jimmy Braun* is one very specific child.

So what we have in the paragraph on stress are general points, such as fear and anxiety, plus examples, such as fear of the dark and anxiety about grades, that we might call generalized examples (not really specific).

This is a paragraph of *classification*—it gives us kinds of stress. But isn't it also in a way a paragraph of *definition*? By giving us the different kinds of stress, and many examples, doesn't it explain to us what stress is?

EXERCISE 16   Answering Questions on "Stress"

1. When reading your textbooks, it is always important to distinguish between the general idea and the example. With the list below, decide whether each item from the paragraph on stress is a *general point or idea* or whether it is an *example*. Label each one G, for general, or E, for example.

   A. _____ fear   D. _____ a quarrel

   B. _____ unfriendly dogs   E. _____ stress from serious matters

   C. _____ passing stress   F. _____ divorce

2. One of the *kinds* of stress we have read about is stress from everyday happenings. Several examples are given, such as bad traffic, or a storm (sentence 6). Now *give*

   an example of your own of stress from everyday happenings. _____

   _____

3. Two kinds of serious events described in sentences 7 and 8 cause stress. Read both sentences again. The examples in sentence 8 are different from those in sentence 7.

   How are they different? _____

   _____

4. Sentence 9 repeats the first part of sentence 1. Read the two sentences again, numbers 9 and 1. Why do you suppose the writer *repeats* in this way? Choose the best answer.
   A. to bring us back to the main point of the paragraph
   B. to make us remember the words
   C. to repeat, just to repeat   Which one? _____

5. The conclusion of a paragraph may do one of many things. For example, it may
   A. summarize the paragraph
   B. repeat the main point of the paragraph
   C. simply give us an idea of what the next topic will be
   D. add a new, somewhat different point on the same topic

   The final sentence of the paragraph on stress does one of these things. Which? Does it summarize? Or what? There are two possible answers, but one is probably better.
                                        Which one would you choose? _____

WOMEN'S STUDIES   Mary McLeod Bethune

As we look at the history of our nation, we read about such famous women as the heroic Harriet Tubman, an antislavery fighter who helped more than three hundred slaves escape; Eleanor Roosevelt, lecturer, writer, and diplomat; and Mary McLeod Bethune, educator and political leader.

Mary McLeod Bethune was born in 1875 of a poor family, with few prospects. As a woman and as a black, she had no reason to expect a life full of achievement and satisfaction.

Mary McLeod Bethune began her adult life quietly as a graduate of the Moody Bible Institute. Before her death at the age of 80, this child of freed slaves had received honorary degrees from several universities, as well as honors such as the Spingarn Medal and the Thomas Jefferson Award. Hers was a long life of service to education and to the nation. During her years as president of Bethune-Cookman College, she acted as director of the Division of Negro Affairs of the National Youth Administration, and organized the National Council of Negro Women. A strong believer in Constitutional guarantees of religious freedom, she was a founding member of Americans United for Separation of Church and State. During World War II, she served as special assistant to the Secretary of War, and was a consultant on interracial matters for the United States in the conference which organized the United Nations. Dr. Bethune is outstanding in American history as an example of dedication to education and public service. A memorial statue to her stands in a public park in the nation's capital. It shows her as a regal figure handing a scroll—a symbol of knowledge—to two children who stretch out their hands to receive it.

EXERCISE 17   Answering Questions on "Mary McLeod Bethune"

1. As we finish reading the paragraph, we can visualize the statue showing Dr. Bethune handing the scroll of knowledge to two children, who hold out their hands to receive it. Why is it appropriate to show Dr. Bethune passing on the scroll of knowledge to children?

   _____

   _____

2. A. When did Dr. Bethune die? The opposite page gives you the information that

      you need to figure this out. Dr. Bethune died in the year _____

   B. The statue referred to was placed in a Washington, D.C., park one hundred years after her birth, in an impressive public ceremony. This statue was erected

      in the year _____

3. Dr. Bethune's many achievements make Americans look up to her. Of the achievements mentioned, select two that *you* think are impressive.

   A. _____

   B. _____

4. What we have is a factual account of Dr. Bethune's life. But from this factual account we can guess what some of her personal concerns, qualities, and abilities must have been. Put a check (✓) beside each of the qualities listed below that would probably apply. CAUTION: Omit those that might apply but that you have no real basis for knowing about. For example, she might have been interested in conservation, but this factual account gives us no real reason for thinking so.

   _____ organizational ability
   _____ special concern for the elderly
   _____ interest in young people
   _____ concern for interracial affairs
   _____ selfishness

   _____ considerable intelligence
   _____ concern for herself as an individual
   _____ ability to work with other people
   _____ scholarship in American history
   _____ concern for black women
   _____ unselfishness
   _____ tendency to worry

5. The Bethune paragraph begins with an introductory sentence or two. Copy below the sentence that states the main idea of the paragraph.

   _____

   _____

   _____

EDUCATION   An Urban Community College

A community-college catalogue provides us with this paragraph. Note that some words are defined in a brief glossary following the paragraph.

[1]An urban community college generally offers its students a variety of two-year vocational curricula, ranging from nursing to photography to secretarial science. [2]Each two-year curriculum requires approximately sixty hours of credit, or four full semesters of college work. [3]These two-year programs lead to an A.A. degree or certificate from the college. [4]Many students find the vocational programs helpful in broadening their education, since all require some courses such as English and sociology; moreover, such programs are designed to lead into specific job opportunities. [5]Other students attend community colleges to enter transfer programs, earning credits that may be transferred to baccalaureate institutions for application toward a B.A. degree. [6]A student who has selected a transfer institution should discuss his plans with his curriculum adviser or counselor. [7]It may also be advisable to visit the transfer institution, study its catalogue, and consult its admissions office. [8]The acceptance of transfer credits is the prerogative of the receiving institution. [9]Because the urban community college offers both two-year vocational curricula and transfer programs, it attracts a variety of students.

A.A.   Associate in Arts, a two-year
　　　degree
B.A.   Bachelor of Arts, a four-year
　　　degree
B.S.   Bachelor of Science, a four-year
　　　degree
baccalaureate   awarding the B.A. or
　　　B.S. degree

curriculum (plural, *curricula*)   a planned
　　　series of courses leading to
　　　specialization
prerogative   a special privilege
vocational   pertaining to preparation for
　　　an occupation

EXERCISE 18   Answering Questions on "An Urban Community College"

1. This paragraph explains two kinds of college programs or credits.
   A. Sentences 1 through 4 explain the first kind of program. Read these sentences over quickly. How would you describe this kind of program?

   _____

   B. Sentence 5 through 8 explain a second kind of program. How would you describe this kind?

   _____

2. These two parts of the paragraph are both closely related to the overall topic of the

   paragraph, which is _____

3. The paragraph begins with four sentences explaining the first kind of program; then we read about the second kind. Yet there is a topic sentence, which mentions both kinds of programs and also states the main idea of the paragraph. This is

   sentence number _____

4. Sentence 4 mentions two advantages of the two-year vocational programs.
   A. Which of the two advantages would most students consider more important, do you think? (Reread the sentence if you need to.)

   The important advantage for most students, in my opinion, would be _____

   _____

   B. What is the other advantage? _____

   _____

5. Suppose that you are studying at a community college. You hope to transfer to Whitby College to earn a B.A. in art. Why, in your opinion, would it be advisable for you to study the Whitby catalogue and perhaps even visit Whitby College?

   _____

   _____

   _____

6. If you were taking an education course and were studying about community colleges, your instructor might ask you this question:

   Why do a variety of students attend urban community colleges?

   In the first sentence of your answer, echo the question, saying something like "A variety of students attend community colleges because . . ." Then explain why.

   _____

   _____

   _____

   _____

   _____

   _____

   _____

PSYCHOLOGY   Authority

This paragraph on authority is similar in some ways to the one on stress (see page 96) and is also from the field of psychology. But there is one important difference. Here we have really specific examples: Tommy, Miss Ross, Sergeant Butz. These are not generalized examples. On the contrary, they are quite specific; they refer to specific individuals.

We might note two words of interest. One is *cope*. Let's define it by using examples. We cope with our teachers, and with measles or a bad cold. We cope with life situations, such as missing the bus, taking a final exam, or getting married. We deal with these, handle them somehow or other. This is coping.

The second word, *reprimand*, is just a fancy word for scold.

[1]All of us must learn to cope with authority. [2]But it's not easy. [3]When four-year-old Tommy didn't get the ice cream he wanted because, as his father explained, it would spoil his appetite for dinner, how did Tommy react? [4]Did he say, "You're right, Dad"? [5]Not likely! [6]Two years later, in first grade, Miss Ross gave instructions to him—in the classroom, in the playground. [7]Tommy tried to be patient and do as he was told, but it was hard. [8]Even Mrs. Johnson, the librarian in the town library, had rules she wanted him to follow. [9]As he grew into a teenager, Tommy's problem with authority became greater. [10]Now he would sometimes lose his temper and complain loudly, "Dad, why *can't* I have the car?" [11]And he found it harder to be polite when Mr. Perez, the neighborhood police officer, found it necessary to reprimand him. [12]Some of the laws he had to follow weren't easy to bear: his town, for example, had a midnight curfew for teenagers. [13]That was hard to take! [14]But the worst of the authority problem was yet to come. [15]When Tom was nineteen, he enlisted in the United States Army. [16]His sergeant, Sergeant Butz, was a believer in strict discipline. [17]He was tough, almost as tough as a man Tom met after he left the Army—Mr. A. G. Wilson, the man who gave him his first real job, and who is still his boss.

Before going on, glance back over the paragraph, noticing the number of specific examples. "His father" is the first specific example: Tommy's father—one specific man. Notice the others.

EXERCISE 19   Answering Questions on "Authority"

1. Our overall topic here is coping with authority. Again we have classification: *kinds* of authority and *examples* of each kind. Also, the material in this paragraph is arranged in a certain order. What kind of order?
    A. space order
    B. random order (no special order)
    C. time order   A, B, or C? _____

    There's also the matter of importance. This is sometimes called *rank order*. In this case, serious and significant items, in your opinion, come
    D. first in the paragraph
    E. in the middle of the paragraph
    F. at the end of the paragraph   D, E, or F? _____

2. List below the *kind* of authority referred to in each group of sentences. Be sure to list the *kind* (parental, say), not the *example* (Miss Ross). One kind is repeated.

    A. sentences 3, 4, 5   _____

    B. sentences 6, 7   _____

    C. sentence 8   _____

    D. sentence 10   _____

    E. sentences 11, 12, 13   _____

    F. sentences 15, 16   _____

    G. sentence 17   _____

3. Examples are given of each kind of authority. In sentences 11, 12, and 13, we have two examples, one a person and one not. Both are specific. These are:

    _____ and _____

4. There are two quotations in the paragraph, but only one sounds real. Which one sounds like a real-life remark? Something Tommy might actually have said under the circumstances?
    A. "You're right, Dad."
    B. "Dad, why *can't* I have the car?"   A or B? _____

5. Sentences 1 and 2 introduce the paragraph. Notice that in question 2 many sentence numbers are given, but numbers 9 and 14 are omitted. *Reread* sentences 9 and 14. Which of the statements below explains their usefulness in the paragraph?
    A. They give specific examples.
    B. They are personal opinions the writer wants to express.
    C. They are transitional sentences that make the paragraph easier to read.

                                                            A, B, or C? _____

MEDICINE   Weight Loss

Patient #12 is a 36-year-old woman, 5′ 3″ tall, weighing 230 pounds. Her ideal weight is 125.

We can calculate 2,040 calories as a maintenance diet, one on which her weight will remain the same. This figure includes a 20% allowance for average activity. We must provide fewer calories in order to accomplish a weight loss. On an 800-calorie diet, the patient will have a daily calorie deficit of 1,240 calories (2,040 − 800). She can be expected to lose on an average some 2.5 pounds weekly, as shown in the figure. At the end of nine weeks, she should weigh 207.5 pounds. Her rate of weight loss will be calculated again every nine weeks.

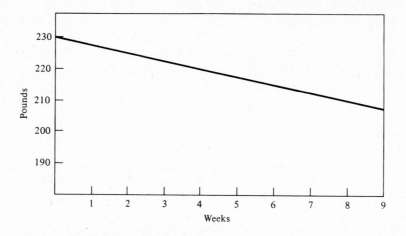

Rate of Weight Loss of Patient #12 on an 800-Calorie Diet

The 800-calorie diet will provide:

Breakfast		*Noon Meal*		*Evening Meal*	
Fruit	1 serving	Meat	2 ounces	Meat	3 ounces
Egg	1	Vegetable	1 serving	Vegetable	1 serving
Toast	1 slice	Salad	1 serving	Salad	1 serving
Beverage	1 cup	Fruit	1 serving	Fruit	1 serving
		Beverage	1 cup	Beverage	1 cup

At this rate of loss, there should be no unfortunate side effects on the patient's overall health.

Total weight loss will be 105 pounds. A period with no loss, on a maintenance diet, may be arranged between periods of weight loss. The total weight loss thus may be accomplished in some forty weeks, more or less, or may be spread out over a year or more.

From "The Prediction of Weight Loss on a Reducing Diet" by John F. Briggs, M.D., Arthur Wells, M.D., and Henry G. Moehring, M.D. Published in *Minnesota Medicine* (April 1960) and reprinted in the *Mayo Clinic Diet Manual*, 4th ed. (W. B. Saunders, 1971). Used by permission of *Minnesota Medicine*, the Mayo Clinic, and Arthur Wells, M.D.

EXERCISE 20   Answering Questions on "Weight Loss"

1. The patient described is referred to as #12, rather than by name. She is
    A. an example, not a real person
    B. a real person
    C. either—we can't tell for sure   A, B, or C? _____

2. What is a maintenance diet? A maintenance diet _____

    _____

3. Patient #12 needs 2,040 calories daily just to maintain her present weight. She'll
    get 800 calories daily, which is 1,240 less than she needs for weight maintenance.
    Thus she gets
    A. more than 1/3 of what she needs for maintenance
    B. about 2/3 of what she needs for maintenance
    C. 800/1240 of what she needs for maintenance   A, B, or C? _____

4. At the end of the fourth week, how many pounds will our patient have lost? She'll

    have lost approximately _____ pounds.

5. On the 800-calorie diet, the evening meal is more satisfying than the noon meal

    only because _____

6. This question deals with matters of personal feeling.
    A. If you yourself were 105 pounds overweight, like #12, would you, do you think,

        be willing to go on such a diet?   Yes or no? _____

    B. If you were determined to lose 105 pounds, would you be willing to spread the
        weight loss over as long a time as forty weeks or a year?

                                            Yes or no? _____

PSYCHOLOGY   Behavior

Sometimes we behave without thinking, as when we pull our hands back from a flame. We don't stop to think about it. At other times our behavior does involve thinking.

Here is a table that shows types of behavior by plants, animals, and human beings. Read it through.

As you look at the last example, it's helpful to remember three meanings:

geo-   earth   *photo-*   light   *hydro-*   water

Types of Behavior

Type	Description	Examples
Intelligent behavior	Thought and memory needed	Solving a problem; writing a letter; farm dog rounding up cattle
Habitual behavior	Repeated action that satisfies a need	Brushing teeth; habitual exercise
Trial-and-error learning	Errors gradually removed after many trials	Using a typewriter; driving a car
Conditioned response	Learned behavior	Child answering to its name; child or dog responding to the command "No!"
Instinct	No thought involved; inborn behavior	Newborn baby or puppy nursing; beaver building dam; lioness teaching her young to hunt
Reflex	Inborn behavior	Blinking eyes at dust; pulling hand back from fire
Tropism	Inborn behavior; turning toward a stimulus	Phototropism: leaves and moths Geotropism: roots Hydrotropism: roots

As scientists study more and more animals, they discover that many species follow complicated behavior patterns. Bird songs and the behavior of bees have been studied for years. Dolphins have an interesting communication system that is being studied. Much of animal communication is instinctive. In human beings, communication in speech or writing is learned, intelligent behavior.

EXERCISE 21   Answering Questions on "Types of Behavior"

1. According to the table, plant roots automatically seek out or turn *toward* two things (positive tropism).

   These are _____ and _____

2. If, during a physical examination, the doctor taps your knee, it will jerk. Would this be a reflex, intelligent behavior, or a habit?

   It is _____

3. Deerflies, unlike common houseflies, have wings with an interesting and even an attractive pattern. Unfortunately, their bite causes smarting and pain. When a person acquires a fear of deerflies, this is
   A. a conditioned response
   B. a tropism
   C. a reflex   Which, A, B, or C? _____

4. Many children gradually learn how to get an angry mother or father into a better mood. They usually find this out by
   A. instinct
   B. trial-and-error learning
   C. reflex   A, B, or C? _____

5. The table lists for us a few common habits. Give another example of your own.

   _____

   _____

6. Some dogs learn to ring doorbells in order to be let into the house. There are two headings under which you might classify this; one is *trial-and-error learning*; the other is *intelligent behavior*.

   Which do you favor? _____
   It would be interesting to see how many of your classmates agree with your answer.

7. Human communication by speech or writing is intelligent behavior. How would you classify the dolphin's system of communicating signals? Consider carefully.

   _____

BOTANY   Color Inheritance in Many Flowering Plants

In the diagram, the letter R indicates a plant with red flowers, the letter W represents a plant with white flowers, and the letter P indicates a plant with pink flowers.

Four generations of plants are shown in this simplified diagram. Follow the progress of the color distribution in all four. As we look at the fourth generation, it's clear how the pattern repeats itself.

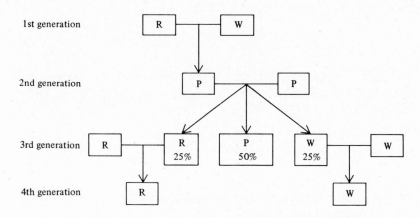

Color Inheritance in Many Flowering Plants

Can you see how plant developers select plants for cross-fertilization? Suppose you want a plant that will produce not the usual pink flower, but one that is a very light, faint pink. You select, first, a pink-flowering plant and a white-flowering plant for cross-fertilization. Next, you take a second-generation pink-flowering plant, which is closer to what you want, and cross-fertilize it with another white-flowering plant. You continue this process until you have exactly the shade of very pale pink that you have in mind.

Plants can, of course, be selected for other qualities than color. Examples of desirable qualities might be resistance to insects or ability to survive low winter temperatures. Perhaps the aim is the fruit of the plant—a larger apple, a tastier plum. A flower with a strong scent can be bred to have no fragrance at all.

The same kind of selective breeding has been done with animals, like sheep and cattle. Such careful scientific work has benefited all of us.

EXERCISE 22   Answering Questions on
"Color Inheritance in Many Flowering Plants"

1. The chart shows that cross-fertilizing one R (red-flowering) and one W
   (white-flowering) plant in the first generation produces pink flowers in the second.
   If the R and W plants shown in the fourth generation were cross-fertilized,
   the flowers of the fifth generation would be what color?

   _____

2. Two pink-flowering plants can produce
   A. only pink-flowering plants
   B. plants bearing pink, red, or white flowers
   C. plants exactly like the parent plants   Which? _____

3. The descendants of two pink-flowering plants might be red, white, or pink. The
   pink-flowering plants would be—check the chart on this—
   A. 100 percent of the total number
   B. 50 percent of the total number
   C. 25 percent of the total number   Which? _____

4. According to the passage, plants can be selected and cross-fertilized for other
   qualities in addition to color.
   Mention two desirable qualities you might try to achieve by selective
   cross-fertilization.

   A. _____

   B. _____

5. The passage mentions selective breeding of several kinds. Check (✓) each kind that
   is mentioned specifically.

   A. _____ trees   D. _____ vegetables

   B. _____ flowering plants   E. _____ fruit

   C. _____ sheep and cattle   F. _____ grass

Geologic Time Chart

MAIN DIVISIONS OF GEOLOGIC TIME			PRINCIPAL PHYSICAL AND BIOLOGICAL FEATURES
ERAS	PERIODS or SYSTEMS		
PRE-CAM-BRIAN	EARLY PRECAMBRIAN* 4,500,000,000		Crust formed on molten earth; history unknown.
	LATE PRECAMBRIAN* 2,000,000,000		History complex and obscure; first evidence of life, algae and invertebrates.
PALEOZOIC	CAMBRIAN 600,000,000		Shallow seas covered parts of continents; first abundant record of marine life.
	ORDOVICIAN 500,000,000		Great expansion among marine invertebrates.
	SILURIAN 425,000,000		Great mountains formed in NW Europe; first small land plants appeared.
	DEVONIAN 405,000,000		Land plants evolved rapidly; primitive fishes; first sharks, insects, and amphibians.
	CARBONIFEROUS	Mississippian 345,000,000	Land plants became diversified, including many kinds of ancient trees; land animals little known.
		Pennsylvanian 310,000,000	Mountains grew along E coast of North America; cockroaches and first reptiles appeared.
	PERMIAN 280,000,000		Great glaciers in S. Hemisphere; conifers present; reptiles surpassed amphibians.
MESOZOIC	TRIASSIC 230,000,000		Ferns and cycads dominant among plants; earliest dinosaurs.
	JURASSIC 180,000,000		Conifers and cycads dominant among plants; primitive birds appeared.
	CRETACEOUS 135,000,000		Rocky Mountains began to rise; most plants, invertebrate animals, fishes, and birds of modern types; dinosaurs reached maximum development, then became extinct; mammals small and very primitive.
		Epochs or Series	
CENOZOIC	TERTIARY	Paleocene 65,000,000	Great development of primitive mammals.
		Eocene 55,000,000	Expansion of early mammals; primitive horses appeared.
		Oligocene 35,000,000	Many older types of mammals became extinct; first monkeys and apes appeared.
		Miocene 25,000,000	Mammals began to acquire modern characters; dogs, modern type horses, manlike apes appeared.
		Pliocene 10,000,000	Much modernization of mammals; first possible apelike men appeared in Africa.
	QUATERNARY	Pleistocene 600,000	Great glaciers covered much of N America and NW Europe; many giant mammals; appearance of modern man late in Pleistocene
		Recent 12,000	Glaciers restricted to Antarctica and Greenland; extinction of giant mammals; development and spread of modern human cultures.

*Regarded as separate eras. All figures indicate approximate number of years since beginning of each division.

algae primitive water plants
amphibian surviving both on land and in water
conifer cone-bearing tree
cycad tree with fernlike foliage

dinosaur large extinct reptile
invertebrate having no backbone
mammal vertebrate; females suckle young
vertebrate having a backbone

Based upon the Geologic Time Chart in *Webster's New World Dictionary of the American Language*, 2nd College Ed. Copyright © 1976 by William Collins & World Publishing Co., Inc.

EXERCISE 23   Answering Questions on "Time"

Before you begin the exercise, read down the right-hand column of the Geologic Time Chart, the one headed "Principal Physical and Biological Features." Physical features would include mountains and seas. Biological features begin with algae and end with modern man.

As you read, note the figures given at the left—the approximate number of years ago that each time period began. Remember that 1,000,000 is one million. The largest number shown is 4,500,000,000, or four and a half billion.

Did you check the glossary under the chart? If not, do that now.

1. The first known life on earth was one-celled algae. When did the first algae appear, according to the chart? Approximately how many years ago? Write the number

   carefully. _____
   Now write the number out in words. How many billion?

   _____

   _____

2. Which of these statements is true?
   A. Life began in the sea and moved to the land.
   B. Life began on land and moved to the sea.
   C. Life began on land and in the sea at the same time.   A, B, or C? _____

3. Humans are vertebrates and mammals. The very first primitive mammals, according

   to the chart, began to appear approximately _____ years ago.

4. The human was an advanced form of mammal. How many years ago, approximately, did advanced or modern mammals begin to appear on earth?

   Approximately _____

5. Modern man appeared later. Approximately when did modern man appear?

   "Late in Pleistocene" might mean about _____ years ago.

6. Was modern man an early arrival or a late arrival, according to the time chart showing the geologic history of the earth?

   Modern man was _____

AMERICAN HISTORY   The Sectional Conflict

This portion of a chapter from an American History textbook discusses three kinds of loyalty, also called feeling, devotion, pride, or affection. Here again an author changes his terms. But if he did not, he'd end up using the word *loyalty* over and over again.

<u>Transitions</u>.   Transitions, as we've seen, are important in textbook reading. Transitional words, like *later*, and transitional phrases, like *as a result*, help us to understand the development of events or ideas. The passage contains a number of transitional sentences. Let's look at one of them.

The first sentence of paragraph 5 is a clear transitional sentence of the kind textbook writers often use. It refers backward, then forward, this way:

⟵⎯⎯⎯⎯⎯⎯⎯   ⎯⎯⎯⎯⎯⟶

The rising nationalist sentiment did not destroy *other loyalties*.

This leads us on to the discussion of the second kind of loyalty, state and local.

<u>Imagination</u>.   Whenever we read any kind of historical passage, or a story that deals with the past, we need to use our imaginations overtime. Here we start with the opening of the nineteenth century—1800 and 1812. Imagine what it would be like to live in a new country that the world generally regarded as a very doubtful experiment in democracy. The new nation, in spite of these doubts, is thriving and prospering and feels proud. And we, like Americans of that day, feel loyal to our cities and states and also to our nation. We have come to regard nearby states as friends and neighbors, part of our section of the country.

<u>Special terms and background information</u>.   There are a few special terms. You probably know that the "Old World Powers" were the European countries. The "lyceum circuit" may be a puzzler, since this kind of popular lecture tour is of little importance in these days of mass-media radio and television.

The words *economic* and *economy* are important. *Economy* refers to the production and distribution of basic goods, such as food. The "plantation economy" produced mostly cotton. Tidewater planters lived in the southeast between the coastal area and the mountains—a rich and fertile land. The Gulf planters lived in the area along the Gulf of Mexico—Alabama, Mississippi, Louisiana.

It may help also to know that the Erie Canal ran east and west between the states of New York and Ohio. The canal made it easy for goods produced in Ohio to be shipped east, instead of having to be sent south along the Ohio and Mississippi rivers. The West in those days was the area just west of the Mississippi.

<u>Following the writer's line of thought</u>.   This is not too difficult to do in the passage on sectionalism. First, we read about national loyalty or patriotism, its sources, how it was encouraged, then the practical reasons why it grew. Next, we have a paragraph on state and local loyalties. Finally, we come to sectional loyalty and to conflict between sections. The first sectional conflict was between the East and the West. Then conflict arose between the North and the South—a conflict that led eventually to the Civil War.

THE SECTIONAL CONFLICT

[1]The expansion of the United States after the War of 1812 greatly increased nationalist feeling in the American republic. Americans were pleased and impressed at the growth of their country, which quadrupled in size between 1800 and 1850. No less impressive was the westward movement, which quickly settled large areas of the newly acquired territory. Citizens were also conscious of the census figures, which showed that the United States was gaining population much more rapidly than the Old World powers. The quick, decisive victory over Mexico was a further source of pride to Americans, as was the flow of European immigrants into the United States. Even those who disliked the newcomers saw in immigration a recognition of the superiority of the United States.

[2]Nor was that all. Americans soaked up patriotism in the schools, where teachers taught their students about the great resources of their country and the glorious deeds of their ancestors. The historians also helped the cause. Biographer Jared Sparks corrected George Washington's spelling errors, lest the General seem a little short of perfect; and George Bancroft treated American history as the story of a chosen people.

[3]The newspapers were filled with similar sentiments (vainglorious boasting, thought European visitors). Longfellow and other poets turned out nationalistic verse, and novelists and philosophers did their patriotic best in prose. Flag-waving orations were popular on the lyceum circuit—Edward Everett's tribute to Washington, for instance—and politicians found it worth their while to be enthusiastic nationalists. From Daniel Webster down to local spellbinders, these politicians praised the nation extravagantly at Fourth of July picnics, on campaign tours, in legislative halls.

[4]Most of the public seemed to like all this, to expect and demand it. Devotion to the nation was emotionally appealing. What was more, it seemed economically logical in a country with a good transportation system and a developing domestic trade. National patriotism also seemed to fit in with the increasing mobility of the American people. A citizen who lived in Pennsylvania all his life might think of himself as primarily a Pennsylvanian. But if he moved west into Ohio, and later to Iowa, he was unlikely to be completely devoted to any of his three states of residence. In all probability, he would consider himself primarily an American.

[5]The rising nationalist sentiment did not destroy other loyalties. In everyday life—in politics, education, and law enforcement—the state and local governments remained the most vital units. Most Americans felt deeply attached to their towns or villages, cities or counties. State pride was also very much in evidence. Many citizens, in fact, managed to be loyal to more than one state. Thus, the Virginian who moved west to Missouri became devoted to his new state without losing any of his affection for the Old Dominion.

[6]Important though they were, state and local loyalties did not provide the nation with its major challenge. That challenge came rather from sectionalism.

From pp. 499–502 in *An American History*, vol. 1, by Merle Curti, Richard H. Shryock, Thomas C. Cochran, and Fred Harvey Harrington. Copyright 1950 by Harper & Row, Publishers, Inc. By permission of the publisher.

The early nineteenth century, which saw the rapid rise of nationalism, also saw a great increase in sectional consciousness. As travel and communication improved, residents of adjacent states became aware of their common interests, and looked at problems in terms of blocs of states. Individuals then came to think of themselves as New Englanders rather than as citizens of Maine or Rhode Island; as Southerners rather than Carolinians or Georgians.

[7]Sectional feeling, grounded in common interests over a large area, developed quickly when political conflicts touched those interests. Thus sectional consciousness in New England was increased by that area's opposition to the War of 1812; and southern sectional consciousness grew during the later slavery controversy. Sectional feeling was most acute when the states involved felt themselves to be a minority group opposed by a majority in the nation.

[8]In studying sections, it must be remembered that sectional lines are not always sharply drawn; that these lines shift from time to time; and that there are subsections or special regions within each section. On some issues, the Ohio of 1840 was part of the North; on others, it belonged to the West. Within the South, there was a sharp contrast between the plantation lowlands and the Appalachian highland area. The hill country, therefore, might or might not cooperate with the rest of the South on a given issue. To increase the complications, class interests cut across sectional lines, as when Jefferson and Jackson won the backing of western farmers and eastern workingmen.

[9]Between 1800 and 1830, an East–West division was the most conspicuous in the country as a whole. Interested in cheap land, easy credit, and improved transportation, the states of the Mississippi Valley were conscious of their common interest as Westerners. They felt tied together, too, by the great Mississippi River, which linked the Northwest with the Southwest, Ohio and Illinois with Louisiana and Alabama. Meanwhile, Easterners felt united in opposition to the West. Tidewater planters of Carolina and Virginia regarded with suspicion the rise of Southwest states like Mississippi and Alabama, and New Englanders viewed the settlement of the Great Lakes region with distaste.

[10]From the 1830s on, the East–West conflicts gradually abated. The construction of roads, canals, and railroads running west across the mountains brought the Northwest back into contact with the Northeast. Thus the Erie Canal shifted the Ohio trade back to New York City, and away from New Orleans. In later decades the railroads tightened the same ties. Sentimental bonds reinforced the economic links, for the Northwest was settled largely by people from the Northeast states. Family connections also helped to unite the Southeast and the Southwest. The expansion of the plantation economy into the Gulf states worked in the same direction, for it put the Southwest and Southeast on one economic plane. Finally, railroads running along east–west lines brought the southeastern states into more effective contact with the Southwest. These developments produced a new sectional alignment. The southeastern and southwestern states, now working together, represented southern interests against the northeastern and northwestern states, now joined in a northern combination.

Generalized Review of " The Sectional Conflict"

In nineteenth-century America, patriotism grew as the country grew in population, in size of the settled areas, and in trade within the country. Teachers and preachers, poets and politicians, all praised the growing nation. In everyday life, Americans also loved their hometowns, their counties, their states. But next to their nation, Americans loved their own section of the country—New England, for example. And there were conflicts between sections, for a while between the East and the West, which was then centered around the Mississippi River. But a longer-lasting conflict arose between the North and the South, whose life styles and ways of earning a living came to be very different. For Southerners, for example, love of the South became almost as great as their love for their country.

A Question for Thought or Discussion

We have read about loyalty to the nation, local loyalties, and loyalty to a section of the country.

How important are each of these loyalties to you and to your family and friends? If you are, say, a Spanish-American or a Swedish-American, or if you are black, is there some feeling of loyalty in addition to those mentioned? Would this be true of one generation and not of another?

EXERCISE 24   Answering Questions on "The Sectional Conflict"

1. Paragraph 1 of the passage consists of a series or list of
   A. kinds of people and institutions that encouraged nationalism during this period
   B. sources of national pride at this time
   C. economic and social reasons why nationalism fitted in with the situation that existed at the time

   Which description fits the list given in paragraph 1?   A, B, or C? _____

2. Paragraphs 2 and 3 contain a list also. Which item from question 1 describes the list in paragraphs 2 and 3?

   A, B, or C? _____

3. Paragraph 4 also contains a list. Which item from question 1 describes this list?

   A, B, or C? _____

4. The first three paragraphs have a number of transitional words and phrases, expressions like "a further source of pride" in paragraph 1. These are designed to remind readers of what has gone before (in this case, other sources of pride) and to prepare them for what comes next.

   Check (✓) *three* of the following sentences in which the underlining indicates a transitional word or phrase relating the sentence to the previous sentence.

   A. _____ No less impressive was the westward movement.

   B. _____ The quick, decisive victory over Mexico was a further source of pride.

   C. _____ Even those who disliked the newcomers saw in immigration a recognition of the superiority of the United States.

   D. _____ Americans soaked up patriotism in the schools.

   E. _____ The historians also helped the cause.

   F. _____ The newspapers were filled with similar sentiments.

5. Paragraph 2 opens with a transitional sentence, not just a word or phrase of transition. The sentence is: "Nor was that all." This sentence means that
   A. the author will now review the material he has just given us
   B. the author will now proceed to a completely different topic
   C. the author will now proceed with the same topic or a closely related topic

   Which one? _____

6. Our writer begins by talking about "nationalist feeling." In the second paragraph he switches to "patriotism," and then uses both "nationalist" and "patriotic" in the third paragraph.

   In the fourth paragraph, he uses two expressions for this same meaning.

   Write *one* of them here. _____

7. Paragraph 6 opens with *two sentences* of transition. The first looks back to the subject of paragraph 5, state and local loyalties. The second transitional sentence

   looks ahead to the topic of paragraph 6, which is _____

8. Choose the statement that best sums up the thought of paragraph 6.
   A. Because of the improvement of travel and communication, nationalism was able to win out over state and local loyalties.
   B. The early nineteenth century saw a rapid rise in nationalism because of our national situation and our many sources of pride.
   C. The main challenge to nationalism came from the growing strength of sectionalism, not from state and local loyalties.

   Which one? _____

9. The relationship of paragraphs 9 and 10 is best expressed this way:
   A. paragraph 10 simply continues 9, listing forces working in the same direction
   B. paragraph 10 stands in contrast to 9, listing forces working in a different direction
   C. paragraph 10 contains an explanation of 9

   Which one of these? _____

10. List in the lefthand column below the three kinds of loyalty discussed in this passage, in the order in which they appear. In the righthand column, give the numbers of the paragraphs in which they are discussed.

    A. _____ in paragraphs _____

    B. _____ in paragraphs _____

    C. _____ in paragraphs _____

11. Which of these three kinds of loyalty will be most important in the chapter of which

    this passage is the first part? _____

ART   Art for Eternity

The next passage, on Egyptian art, is not the opening part of the textbook from which it is taken, *The Story of Art* by E. M. Gombrich. We can tell this from the first and second sentences. Evidently the author has just been discussing, in the previous chapter, primitive art in "the caves of southern France" and the art of "the North American Indians." He calls these "strange beginnings" for art. He tells us that art as we know it began in Egypt.

As textbook writers go from chapter to chapter, they often refer back to what has gone before. Your job is to pick up these references and remember what you have read in earlier chapters. Of course, in this case you can't, because you haven't read the previous chapter. But you can tell that the writer is referring to an earlier discussion.

<u>Special terms</u>.   We all have a picture in our minds of the Egyptian pyramids— "mountains of stone," the author calls them. But do we always think of them as architecture? Probably not, but they are architecture, nevertheless. And architecture is a form of art.

The term *portrait* is used here not for a painting, as we commonly use the word, but for a statue. The statues of Egyptian kings were stone portraits carved in "imperishable granite." The only paintings referred to were on the walls of the king's tomb. The carvings on these stone walls are called *reliefs*. And the magic words and signs with which the dead king's mummy is surrounded are called *spells and incantations*.

Three other special words are *copyist*, *relic*, and *rite*. A copyist is one who copies works of art. A relic is something left over from an earlier time. And a rite is a ceremony or ceremonial custom.

<u>Special problems</u>.   Sometimes the act of visualizing as you read is easy; sometimes it is hard. "A blue sky with fluffy white clouds" calls up a familiar picture. Here you are asked to visualize a certain kind of portrait of a person, carved in stone. This portrait does not show every little line and wrinkle, every tiny detail of dress. That would be what the writer calls "naturalistic." It would be exact, like a photograph. Instead, the portrait is simplified and gives just the basic forms and outlines. Still, it does resemble the person who is portrayed; it is lifelike.

Occasionally in the newspaper we see a satirical drawing making fun of a famous living person. Such a drawing usually uses only a few cleverly drawn lines, but we immediately recognize the person portrayed, even at a glance. Such a drawing is simple yet lifelike.

<u>Following the line of thought</u>.   After the introductory paragraph, we have again a three-part passage, dealing with three kinds of Egyptian art. Watch for the three kinds as you read. And also watch for the basic theme or idea they have in common.

ART FOR ETERNITY

[1]Some form of art exists everywhere on the globe, but the story of art as a continuous effort does not begin in the caves of southern France or among the North American Indians. There is no direct tradition which links these strange beginnings with our own days, but there is a direct tradition, handed down from master to pupil, and from pupil to admirer or copyist, which links the art of our own days, any house or any poster, with the art of the Nile Valley of some five thousand years ago. For we shall see that the Greek masters went to school with the Egyptians, and we are all the pupils of the Greeks. Thus the art of Egypt has a tremendous importance for us.

[2]Everyone knows that Egypt is the land of the pyramids, those mountains of stone which stand like weathered landmarks on the distant horizon of history. However remote and mysterious they seem, they tell us much of their own story. They tell us of a land which was so thoroughly organized that it was possible to pile up these gigantic mounds of stone in the lifetime of a single king, and they tell us of kings who were so rich and powerful that they could force thousands and thousands of workers or slaves to toil for them year in, year out, to quarry the stones, to drag them to the building site, and to shift them with the most primitive means till the tomb was ready to receive the king. No king and no people would have gone to such expense, and taken so much trouble, for the creation of a mere monument. In fact, we know that the pyramids had their practical importance in the eyes of the kings and their subjects. The king was considered a divine being who held sway over them, and on his departure from this earth he would ascend to the gods whence he had come. The pyramids soaring up to the sky would probably help him to make his ascent. In any case they would preserve his sacred body from decay. For the Egyptians believed that the body must be preserved if the soul is to live on in the beyond. That is why they prevented the corpse from decaying by an elaborate method of embalming it, and binding it up in strips of cloth. It was for the mummy of the king that the pyramid had been piled up, and his body was laid right in the center of the huge mountain of stone in a stone coffin. Everywhere round the burial chamber, spells and incantations were written to help him on his journey to the other world.

[3]But it is not only these oldest relics of human architecture which tell of the role played by age-old beliefs in the story of art. The Egyptians held the belief that the preservation of the body was not enough. If the likeness of the king was also preserved, it was doubly sure that he would continue to exist forever. So they ordered sculptors to chisel the king's portrait out of hard, imperishable granite, and put it in the tomb where no one saw it, there to work its spell and to help his soul to keep alive in and through the image. One Egyptian word for sculptor was actually "He-who-keeps-alive."

[4]At first these rites were reserved for kings, but soon the nobles of the royal household had their minor tombs grouped in neat rows around the king's mound; and gradually every self-respecting person had to make provision for his after-life by ordering a costly grave, where his soul could dwell and receive the offerings of food and drink which were given to the dead, and which would house his mummy and his likeness. Some of these early portraits from the pyramid

From *The Story of Art*, by E. H. Gombrich. Reprinted by permission of Phaidon Press Limited.

age . . . are among the most beautiful works of Egyptian art. There is a solemnity and simplicity about them which one does not easily forget. One sees that the sculptor was not trying to flatter his sitter, or to preserve a jolly moment in his life. He was concerned only with the essentials. Every lesser detail he left out. Perhaps it is just because of this strict concentration on the basic forms of the human head that these portraits remain so impressive. For, despite their almost geometrical rigidity, they are not primitive as are the native masks previously discussed. Nor are they as likelike as the naturalistic portraits of the artists of Nigeria. The observation of nature, and the regularity of the whole, are so evenly balanced that they impress us as being lifelike and yet remote and enduring.

[5]This combination of geometrical regularity and keen observation of nature is characteristic of all Egyptian art. We can study it best in the reliefs and paintings that adorned the walls of the tombs. The word "adorned," it is true, may hardly fit an art which was meant to be seen by no one but the dead man's soul. In fact, these works were not intended to be enjoyed. They, too, were meant to "keep alive." Once, in a grim distant past, it had been the custom when a powerful man died to let his servants and slaves accompany him into the grave so that he should arrive in the beyond with a suitable suite. They were sacrificed. Later, these horrors were considered either too cruel or too costly, and art came to the rescue. Instead of real servants, the great ones of this earth were given images as substitutes. The pictures and models found in Egyptian tombs were connected with the idea of providing the souls with helpmates in the other world.

[6]To us these reliefs and wall-paintings provide an extraordinarily vivid picture of life as it was lived in Egypt thousands of years ago. And yet, looking at them for the first time, one may find them rather bewildering.

Generalized Review of "Art for Eternity"

All religions have motivated the artists who believed in them. The great figures of Buddha, with their look of peace, grew out of Buddhism, just as the imposing Hindu temples and sculptures were outpourings of religious faith. This was also true in Egypt.

The divine king of Egypt had to have a suitable monument, which would contain his tomb. It was the duty of the entire nation to see that everything possible was done to help the king's soul ascend to the home of the gods, where it belonged. His people were responsible, and they did the heavy and wearisome work that was required. All during the lifetime of the king, servants and slaves worked and died to build his pyramid. They saw to it that his portrait was carved from long-lasting stone, his body embalmed and sealed in a tomb in the depths of the pyramid, surrounded by paintings, carvings, and magic signs and words. The artists of Egypt were just as much servants of their king as those who toiled to build his monument. Their portraits and paintings, like the pyramids, showed their belief in the divinity of the king, and the need to keep his soul alive after his death. The wall paintings and reliefs showed their belief that these forms of art could keep alive the souls of servants to wait on the king after his death.

A Question for Thought or Discussion

In the life of ancient Egypt, art had a clear and vital function, or use. It served the king and the state religion.

Today, art as we know it does not serve a king, and seldom serves religion. What is the value of art today? What function does it serve? Does it ever serve the nation? Or religion? What value does it have for you?

EXERCISE 25   Answering Questions on "Art for Eternity"

1. The author of this passage states that "*the art of Egypt has a tremendous importance for us.*"
   Which set of phrases below (all from paragraph 1) provides a key to the reason why Egyptian art is so important to us?
   A. does not begin / North American Indians
   B. some form of art / caves of southern France
   C. continuous effort / direct tradition
   D. everywhere on the globe / these strange beginnings   Which one?_____

2. Paragraph 2 tells that the pyramids were useful in two ways to the soul of the dead king. The Egyptians were *sure* of this usefulness in one way and thought the pyramids were *probably* useful in another way.

   Mark with S, for <u>sure</u>, the phrase that applies to the way they felt sure of. Mark with LS, for <u>less sure</u>, the phrase showing the way they weren't really sure of.

   A. _____ to help the king's soul ascend to the home of the gods

   B. _____ to preserve the body of the king from decay

3. Look always for important connections between paragraphs. A sentence, a phrase, or even a word may give you a link, a transition, between the paragraph you have just finished and the one you are about to read.
   A. The first sentence of paragraph 3 refers back to "these oldest relics of human architecture." Which architectural relics has the writer just been talking about

      in paragraph 2?_____
   B. In paragraph 4, the first sentence refers back to "these rites." Which particular

      rites does the writer mean? Check carefully._____

      _____

4. The first sentence in paragraph 3 speaks of "the role played by age-old beliefs in the story of art." To which paragraphs in the essay does this key phrase refer? *Look carefully*. This is very important.
   A. paragraphs 1, 2
   B. paragraphs 2, 3, 4, 5
   C. paragraphs 4, 5, 6   Which, A, B, or C?_____

5. Connections between sentences are important transitions. Let's look at the opening words of two sentences in this passage.

From paragraph 2: "*That is why* they prevented the corpse from decaying by an elaborate method of embalming it."

From paragraph 3: "*So* they ordered sculptors to chisel the king's portrait out of hard, imperishable granite."

Both of these phrases show that
A. what follows *is the opposite* of what has gone before
B. what follows *is the same* as what has gone before
C. what follows *is the result* of what has gone before   Which? _____

6. In paragraph 5, two sentences have opening words or phrases that refer to other periods of time. Write these opening words below.

A. _____

B. _____

7. "Art for Eternity" is concerned with the art of ancient Egypt. The writer, however, refers back to several kinds or periods of art that he evidently has discussed in a previous chapter.

Name *two* of these (see paragraphs 1 and 4).

A. _____

B. _____

8. Paragraph 4 and the first sentence of paragraph 5 tells us of "portraits" that are actually statues—portraits carved in stone. Why does the writer think these are such great art?

Write a well-planned sentence, *using your own words* so far as possible, telling why he thinks they are artistically great.

_____

_____

_____

_____

_____

_____

9. The wall paintings and wall carvings, or reliefs, that adorned the tombs of Egyptian kings are described in paragraph 5.

     What practical use did the Egyptians believe these had? In what way did they help the soul of the dead king? Answer *in your own words*.

_____

_____

_____

_____

10. This passage, taken as a whole, gives an account of three forms of Egyptian art.

    List below the three forms or kinds of art and the numbers of the paragraphs that explain each one. Start with paragraph 2, and go all the way through paragraph 6.

    Form of Art   *Paragraphs*

    A. _____   _____

    B. _____   _____

    C. _____   _____

11. The final paragraph of the passage
    A. is a complete summary of everything that has gone before
    B. is probably a transition to a paragraph telling why the reliefs and wall-paintings are bewildering
    C. states the conclusion the author has reached after studying all three forms of Egyptian art

                              Choose carefully. A, B, or C? _____

STAGE III: ADVANCED READING POWER

BUSINESS   The Industrial Revolution

<u>Organization</u>.   This passage from *An Introduction to Contemporary Business* follows a time sequence, first giving an account of the Industrial Revolution in the United States from 1790 to the Civil War, and then a brief discussion of industrial progress from the Civil War to World War I.

Under the heading "From Independence to the Civil War," we find an analytical approach. The writer examines three aspects of industrial growth: the rise of science and technology, mass production, and improved transportation.

<u>Headings</u>.   Look at the overall title, "The Industrial Revolution." Now turn to the first main heading, "From Independence to the Civil War," which has under it four subheadings, each marked with a √. Next we have another main heading, "From the Civil War to World War I."

Fill in this brief outline, as preparation for reading the passage.

THE INDUSTRIAL REVOLUTION

When you are about to read a textbook chapter, it is an excellent investment of time to preview it, looking at the introduction, the headings, and the conclusion. Making the brief outline on the Industrial Revolution passage should have helped prepare you to read this selection. Did it? You be the judge.

THE INDUSTRIAL REVOLUTION

The *industrial revolution* has been described as "the replacement of hand tools by power-driven machines." Begun in England around 1760, it reached the United States about thirty years later. Typical of the early stages of the industrial revolution was the widespread use of the power loom, the spinning jenny (which permitted simultaneous spinning of several yarns), the machine lathe, and the steamboat.

The industrial revolution: neither wholly industrial nor wholly revolutionary

Ironically, the term "industrial revolution" is misleading in describing the economic and technological events that began in America around 1790 and continue to exert such a profound influence today. First, the revolution was as much agricultural as industrial. During the colonial period farm families comprised more than 95 percent of the population, and even as late as 1850 four out of every five families lived in rural areas (Figure 1–1). Such agricultural innovations as the iron plow, the mechanical planter, and the corn reaper, which were introduced in the 1830s, freed the economy from its overwhelming dependence on the land and made industrial growth possible.

The pace of agricultural progress has accelerated to the present. In the twentieth century output per worker rose twice as fast in agriculture as in industry. By 1971 farmers accounted for only 5 percent of the American population, yet they were able to provide more than enough food for the nonagricultural majority. One of the untold ironies of American history is that after migrating to the United States to find better land, millions of immigrants saw their sons and daughters forced to flock to the cities.

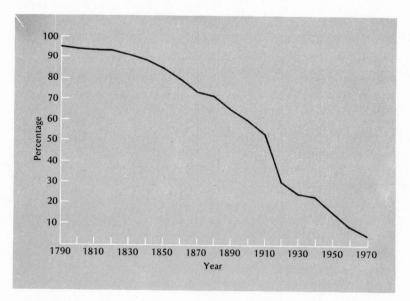

FIGURE 1–1 Percentage of U.S. population in agriculture. (Figures before 1920 include nonfarm rural population.)

Source: *Statistical Abstract of the United States.*

From *An Introduction to Contemporary Business* by William Rudelius, W. Bruce Erickson, and William J. Bakula, Jr., copyright © 1973 by Harcourt Brace Jovanovich, Inc., and reprinted with their permission.

FIGURE 1–2 The industrial revolution in the United States.

THE COLONIAL PERIOD THE INDUSTRIAL REVOLUTION

	1607 Jamestown settled	1790 Industrial revolution in the United States		1939–1945 World War II
	1760 Industrial revolution in England	1812–1815 War of 1812	1914–1918 World War I	
	1776–1783 Revolutionary War	1860–1865 Civil War		1970s
Main economic characteristics	Primitive, largely agricultural economy Transportation by sea and road generally inadequate	Agricultural revolution —development of iron plow, mechanical planter, reaper—beginning in 1830s Rise of science and its extensive use in business Beginning of mass production Improved transportation: turnpikes, canals, clipper ships; introduction of railroad in 1830s; massive wave of railroad construction about 1850	Large-scale production Growth of managerial specialization and scientific management Ford's assembly line Communication greatly improved by widespread use of telegraph, telephone, radio	Chemical revolution Standards and specifications revolution Electronics and automation revolution Energy revolution Extension of genuine mass markets with automobile and truck Computer revolution
Main economic activities	Agriculture, fishing, commerce, fur trading, whaling, banking, land speculation, shipbuilding	Flour and meal milling, cotton goods (textiles), lumber, boats, shoes, men's clothing, iron, leather, woolen goods, yarns	Oil, railroads, steel, mining, meat packing (fur trading and whaling in decline)	Wholesale and retail trade, government and government enterprises, real estate, mining and construction, medical and health services, nonelectrical machinery, agriculture, electrical machinery, food and kindred products, motor vehicles, transportation equipment, primary metals, chemicals

Second, the industrial revolution was as much evolutionary as revolutionary. By contemporary standards the leisurely pace of progress in the nineteenth century is truly astounding; sometimes years elapsed between the discovery of a new scientific principle and its practical application in business.

The industrial revolution, in short, can be viewed as a gradual but accelerating process of change that began in 1790 and extends to the present day. In this sense Americans of the 1970s are both its beneficiaries and its participants. The main sweep of the industrial revolution and its colonial antecedents are illustrated in Figure 1–2.

From Independence to the Civil War

In its formative years the industrial revolution was a product of three interrelated changes: the rise of science and technology, mass production, and improved transportation.

✔ **The rise of science and technology.** Throughout recorded history man's curiosity about the natural world has led him to make a succession of notable scientific discoveries. During the nineteenth century the pace of man's investigation accelerated to an unprecedented degree, particularly in the 1830s and 1840s. These years saw the advent of the telegraph, the mechanical harvester, the sewing machine, the Colt revolver, vulcanized rubber, and a hundred other innovations, all of which were applied to the improvement of everyday life. Samuel F. B. Morse, inventor of the telegraph, established the Magnetic Telegraph Company, the forerunner of Western Union; Cyrus McCormick used his business ability to create the mechanical harvester, the first of International Harvester's many farm implements; and I. M. Singer developed the sewing machine and founded the Singer Company. The modern corporation, with its specialized research laboratories, is a logical continuation of the fruitful cooperation between business and science that evolved during the early stages of the industrial revolution.

The rise of technology: applying science to everyday life

✔ **Mass production.** The foundation for today's system of mass production was laid in 1799, when business pioneer Eli Whitney received a large order for muskets from the U.S. Army. By 1812 Whitney's tiny plant in Hamden, Connecticut, was pouring out muskets in unprecedented quantities by using *interchangeable* or *standard parts* — parts so similar in physical characteristics as to be indistinguishable.

If Whitney invented mass production, Samuel Colt had the foresight to exploit it. Colt, for whom the Colt 45 revolver is named, built the world's first arms factory in Hartford, Connecticut. Colt's production techniques made the manufacture of interchangeable parts so efficient that his factory became known as "America's school for managers."

Mass production: a new approach to increasing output

Mass production is considerably more than the production of goods in quantity; it represents a method of organizing and controlling production in order to increase the physical output of a business. In addition to interchangeable parts, nineteenth-century mass production involved (1) the use of specialized machines to make interchangeable parts feasible; (2) the replacement of human and animal energy by water power, coal, and later oil; and (3) specialization of labor so that workers were assigned a specific set of tasks at which they were skilled. *Standardized products,* goods of uniform and generally high quality, were made possible by the efficiency of nineteenth-century mass production techniques.

Mass production was greatly improved by the *moveable assembly line,* introduced by Henry Ford in the early twentieth century. Ford, observing that a typical worker in a metal shop spent most of his time moving materials from job to job, had a flash of insight one day: Why not send the job to the man rather than the man to the job? In 1913 Ford's Highland Park plant introduced the moveable assembly line, in which incomplete products were carried past men and machines whose positions were fixed and who performed carefully specified operations on the products as they passed on to the next stage. The moveable assembly line quickly became the heart of twentieth-century mass production.

The rise of the factory system

With the advent of mass production in the nineteenth and early twentieth centuries the *factory system* was born. Men and machines were gathered in large manufacturing establishments, known as factories or plants. A business (or firm) might own and operate a single plant or a complex of plants distributed throughout the world. The factory system was so successful at providing goods of comparatively high quality at reasonable prices that it quickly replaced the older *hand-craft system,* with its highly skilled craftsmen employed in small shops.

✔ **Improved transportation.** The Constitution took the first decisive step toward creating mass markets by granting the federal government sole authority to regulate trade between the states. Over the centuries the United States became what has been called "the world's greatest Common Market."

In the early 1800s, however, the problem was not legal but physical —the inability to transport goods over a long distance at a reasonable cost. Roads were exceedingly primitive, and ships could reach only those along the coasts. Quick to recognize the problem, federal and state governments first subsidized a round of frenzied road construction and later embarked on a frantic race to build canals, several of which proved financially disastrous. Steamboats and the famous clipper ships substantially improved water transportation.

Railroads and automobiles led the way to mass markets

But it was the advent of the railroads in 1830, especially the second wave of railroad construction around 1850, that heralded modern mass markets. The changes brought about by the railroads were swift and dramatic; by 1863 Civil War armies and their supplies were largely transported by rail. The famous golden spike ceremony of May 10, 1869, symbolized more than the completion of the first transcontinental railroad: it presaged the beginning of a genuine mass market in the United States.

A transportation system capable of reaching nearly every American consumer had to await the 1920s, when Henry Ford's Model T gave the majority of the population in small towns and rural America effective access to urban centers. The contribution of the automobile to mass marketing—and hence mass production—is inestimable.

The struggling U.S. economy faced a chronic shortage of capital . . .

. . . and lack of a reliable paper currency

✔ **Weaknesses of the pre-Civil War economy.** Despite notable progress in the post-Revolutionary War period, the United States was handicapped by its inadequate financial base. Capital was in extremely short supply, and eventually more than half the money needed to finance American farms and factories was borrowed from England. Currency shortages were chronic, and private banks were permitted to issue their own (often worthless) paper bills. As a result of America's weak financial structure, a series of *panics*—sharp recessions in economic activity— descended like the plague about every five years.

From the Civil War to World War I

The post-Civil War era in the United States has been described as "the age of electricity" or "the age of Edison." This was one of the most exciting periods in human history, with progress bursting forth almost everywhere. Especially noteworthy were the advances in the processing of industrial raw materials and in mass communication. The Bessemer process and its refinements revolutionized steel production, making this industry central to all modern economies until well into the twentieth century. Widespread use of the telegraph, the telephone, and later the radio ushered in an era of instantaneous communication, with shattering long-term economic and social consequences. Equally spectacular improvements in mass production and in transportation marked the era.

The age of electricity and mass communication

In short, the industrial revolution was a cumulative process. The three basic changes that spurred the revolution—science, mass production, and improved transportation—continued to operate after the Civil War with undiminished intensity.

EXERCISE 26   Answering Questions on "The Industrial Revolution"

1. Looking at Figure 1–1, on page 128, we see the decline of farm population in the United States. Compare the decline (A) between 1790 and 1850 with the decline

   (B) between 1890 and 1950. Which was the more rapid decline, A or B?_____

2. We are told that during the early stages of the industrial revolution, a period marked by the rise of science and technology, there was cooperation between business and science. Give two concrete results of this cooperation between business and science—the names of two specific companies that were organized.

   A. _____

   B. _____

3. At the time of the Revolutionary War in 1776, fur trading and whaling were important in the national economy. According to Figure 1–2, on page 129, when

   did these begin to decline in importance?_____

4. Mass production as we know it today was developed gradually, with help from many contributors.

   A. About 1812, Eli Whitney contributed _____

   B. In 1913, Henry Ford contributed _____

5. If you yourself were to invent a successful new gadget today, it would be rapidly and efficiently manufactured by mass production and the factory system. Before the industrial revolution, how would your new gadget have been produced?

   _____

6. A. Improved transportation has affected our lives greatly. To you, as an average American today, which is the most important of the kinds of transportation mentioned in the passage? Steamboats, railroads, or the automobile of the

      1920s?_____

   B. Are airplanes (not mentioned in the passage) even more important to you?

      Yes or no?_____

WORD ROUNDUP

WORDS AND THE DICTIONARY

A large vocabulary—what a great idea! All of us, of course, would like to have an impressive vocabulary. But we must build as we go along, because acquiring a large vocabulary is a long-term process.

As you go on in college, you will gradually increase your mastery of more and more words, sometimes with considerable effort, sometimes quite painlessly, even unconsciously. It will help to become aware that longer words are usually made up of several parts—and to become aware of what some of these parts mean.

First, let's take *a practical approach.* Your most immediate need is to master the important terms in the courses you are taking right now. You must select the terms you want to understand thoroughly and learn how to use well: that's the first step. Your textbook might define these terms, or your instructor might define them. Often, though, you will also need a dictionary. Key terms like *atom* and *molecule* in a science course, for example, are words you must quickly gain a complete understanding of. For help, you have your textbook, you instructor, and your dictionary.

In your leisure reading, on weekends or during summer vacations, you will enlarge your general vocabulary as you read what appeals to you. Don't think you must read something difficult to build your vocabulary. Newspapers, magazines, the latest paperback—all will make a contribution.

But back to the practical approach. Your college library will have the large *Webster's Third International,* called the *Unabridged,* which you may want to consult sometimes. The library will also have such college-level dictionaries as *The Random House Dictionary* and the college edition of *Webster's New World Dictionary.* It is desirable to own a good college dictionary of this kind, for use when studying at home. But you can always use those in the library.

In the section that follows, the words for study have *not* been chosen primarily for vocabulary-building. Instead, they have been selected because they illustrate specific principles of English word structure or pronunciation. Knowing how to pronounce a word is an essential part of mastering the word.

USING YOUR DICTIONARY

Why do you need to use a dictionary? College students, in particular, need their dictionaries for several reasons.

<u>Pronunciation</u> is one reason. Words are spoken sounds or combinations of sounds. Printed words represent these sounds, and knowing how to pronounce them is an important part of understanding the word.

Suppose, for example, that you are taking a music course and are studying certain patterns in music described as

antiphonal

Now, you may think the word looks as if it should be spoken *anti + phone + all*. But in this case the stress, or accent, falls on the *tiph* part, which rhymes with *if*.

Are you going to recognize the word when your instructor says an*tiph*onal? Are you going to embarrass yourself by mispronouncing the word when you recite in class?

Mastery of a word always—but always—includes knowing how to pronounce it. Pronunciation, then, is one reason for using the dictionary.

<u>Meanings</u> of words are another major reason for needing a dictionary. College textbooks always seem to have a number of words that are unfamiliar to us. And some of them look difficult at first glance.

Now, the question is, which words are you going to look up? You probably can't take time to look up and really study every word you don't know. How do you decide?

<u>Emphasize concept words!</u> Words representing a concept or idea that's important for the subject you're studying—these are number one. For example, in a biology or botany course, a key word, an idea word, is

photosynthesis

Photo means "light." Plants manufacture, or *synthesize*, their food with the help of light. You know the word element *photo* from words like "photograph," meaning a picture made with the help of light.

How is the word pronounced? With a heavy stress, or accent, on the *syn* syllable, pronounced *sin*—photo*syn*thesis. Mastering such idea words is basic in a subject-matter course like biology.

In college, you'll be coming across many new terms. Which ones are the concept or idea words, the ones you really need to know? And which ones are less important? You must make this decision.

<u>Special rules</u> are followed for dictionary entries, and every entry is set up according to these rules.

First we have the entry word printed in darker type, and with centered dots between syllables.

re·cord   con·vict   re·fuse

Next we have some symbols for pronunciation, which are explained in a key appearing at the bottom of each righthand page of the dictionary. And then are listed the various meanings of the word, arranged according to parts of speech.

For the word *record*, we begin with the abbreviation *v.t.*, for transitive verb, or one with an object—*number* in this sentence:

> Let's record that number.

How would you pronounce *record* in that sentence? The sound is the same when you use it as a *v.i.*, or intransitive verb (no object), as in "Let's record now."

Now we'll go to *n.*, for noun.

> That's my favorite record.

Hear the difference in sound? The part of speech often makes a difference in pronunciation. Listen to the verb *convict*, then to the noun *convict*.

> Will they convict him?   The convict escaped.

So—the part of speech is important in a dictionary entry.

"CAUTION — *Use Only As Directed*." Make this your motto in using dictionaries. They can be tricky. They don't agree sometimes, even on such a simple matter as how to pronounce a word. They may give you an out-of-date pronunciation or meaning. And they sometimes don't have the newest (and perhaps the most interesting) words.

So use with caution—but *use*. A good dictionary is an essential tool for a college student.

Our first dictionary exercise will deal with *meanings*: the various meanings of the word *fair*, which can be an adjective, a noun, an adverb, or a verb.

A SAMPLE DICTIONARY ENTRY: the word *fair*

Here's a typical dictionary entry. As you read it through slowly, note that it is divided according to parts of speech: adjective (adj.); noun (n.); adverb (adv.); intransitive and transitive verb (v.i. and v.t.).

fair (fâr), *adj.* **1.** attractive, beautiful: *a fair woman.*   **2.** light in color, blond: *a fair-haired child.*   **3.** clear, sunny, said of weather.   **4.** just and honest: *a fair judge.*   **5.** according to the rules: *a fair defeat.*   **6.** likely, promising: *he is in a fair way to make money.*   **7.** of moderately good value or ability: *a fair job.*   **8.** lawfully hunted: *fair game.*   —*n.* **9.** a festival where there is entertainment and things are sold, usually for charity: *a church fair.*   **10.** an exhibition or showing of farm, household, and manufactured products, usually with amusements and educational displays: *the county fair.*   **11.** *Archaic.* a pretty woman.   —*adv.* **12.** in a fair manner: *to play fair.*   **13.** straight, squarely: *struck fair in the face.*   —*v.i.* **14.** *Dial.* to become clear, said of the weather.   —*v.t.* **15.** to smooth, said of wood, etc.

EXERCISE 1   Analyzing the Uses of the Word *fair*

The first four sentences below use *fair* as an adjective (*adj.*). *Fair* is a noun (*n.*) in sentence 5. In 6 we have it as an adverb (*adv.*), and in 7 as a transitive verb (*v.t.*), with *surface* as its object. In the right-hand column, fill in the number of the correct definition from the dictionary entry.

Part of speech		*Definition*
adj.	1. I hope that Sunday will be fair for our picnic.	_____
adj.	2. John cheats at cards, but Harry plays a fair game.	
adj.	3. His grades this semester were only fair, no more. Notice that in sentence 3 *fair* has a less positive or hopeful meaning than in 4. Keep this in mind.	_____
adj.	4. I really believe there's a pretty fair chance of making it.	_____
n.	5. The country fair displayed a lot of farming equipment.	_____
adv.	6. He hit the target fair in the middle.	_____
v.t.	7. We faired the surface with plane and steel wool.	_____

Definition 11 is labeled *Archaic.* This means no longer in general use. (*Thou* is an archaic form of you, for example.) Definition 14 is labeled *Dial.*, for dialect. In standard written English, dialect forms are generally not used.

PRONUNCIATION KEY: a*ct,* ā*ble,* d*âre,* ärt; e*bb,* ē*qual;* i*f,* īce; h*ot,* ōver, ôrder, oil, out; up, ûrge, ūse; b͝oͤok, b͞oͤot; ə = a in *alone;* sin͡g; ͬshoe; ͭthin, ͭthat; c͡hief; kept; go; just; z͡h = s in *measure*

A SAMPLE DICTIONARY ENTRY: the word *dash*

What's *in* a dictionary? As one step toward an answer, let's look at another typical entry.

dash (dash), *v.t.*   **1.** to throw or thrust violently or suddenly.   **2.** to strike violently, esp. so as to break to pieces.   **3.** to splash, to spatter (with mud, water, etc.).   **4.** to apply roughly, as by splashing.   **5.** to mix by adding another substance: *to dash wine with water.*   **6.** to ruin or frustrate (hopes, plans, etc.).   **7.** to depress, dispirit.   **8.** to accomplish quickly: *to dash off a letter.*   —*v.i.* **9.** to strike with violence.   **10.** to move with violence.   **11.** to dash off, to hurry away: *I must dash off now.*   **12.** to dash down, sketch, etc., hastily.   —*n.* **13.** the splashing of a liquid against something.   **14.** the sound of such splashing.   **15.** a small quantity of anything thrown or mixed with something else: *a dash of salt.*   **16.** a hasty stroke, esp. of a pen.   **17.** the sign (—) used to note an abrupt pause in a sentence or utterance, to begin and end a parenthetic word, etc.   **18.** a sudden or impetuous movement; a sudden rush.   **19.** *Track.* a short race: *a 50-yard dash.*   **20.** spirited or lively action; vigor in action or style.   **21.** a dashboard in a car.   **22.** *Telegraphy.* a signal of longer duration than a dot, as in Morse code.   **23.** *Archaic.* a violent, rapid blow or stroke. [ME *dassh(en)*, prob. < ON; cf. Dan *daske* = flap, Sw *daska*]   —*Syn.* **11.** dart, bolt.   **15.** pinch, bit; touch, tinge; suggestion, soupçon.   **20.** flourish.

Notice the labels. Definition 19 is labeled *Track.* 22 is marked *Telegraphy*, and in 23 we meet again our old friend *Archaic.*

Notice, too, that synonyms for definition 11 are *dart* and *bolt*. These apply only to definition 11, "to dash off, to hurry away." Synonyms for definitions 15 and 20 are also given.

The pronunciation key, at the bottom of this page, tells us what we already know— that the *a* in *dash* is pronounced like the *a* in *act*, and that the *sh* is pronounced as it is in *shoe*.

EXERCISE 2   Analyzing the Uses of the Word *dash*

Now we'll work with the entry. Check back carefully for the answer to each question. (In the exercises, S = subject; V = verb; O = object)

1. The abbreviation *v.t.* means transitive verb—a verb that takes an object.

    I dashed off a letter to the registrar.
    S V   O

How many definitions are given for *dash* as a transitive verb?   _____

2. The abbreviation *v.i.* means intransitive verb—a verb that does *not* take an object.

We dashed to the door. (The phrase "to the door" tells *where*, not *what*.)
S   V

How many definitions are given for *dash* as an intransitive verb?   _____

3. The abbreviation *n.* means noun. All the remaining definitions are noun definitions. (Nouns generally are subjects or objects.)

This ended his dash for freedom.   His dash for freedom ended then.
S   V   O   S   V

Notice that the definition that fits these two sentences is number 18.

4. Which definition would fit the meaning of *dash* in these sentences?

A. *v.t.* I must dash off some notes.   _____

B. *v.i.* Let's dash off to class.   _____

C. *n.* Joe won the hundred-yard dash.   _____

D. *n.* Please put in just a dash of whiskey.   _____

E. *n.* He made a dash for the door.   _____

Do you have all the definition numbers written in on the right?

The part of a dictionary entry shown in brackets [ ] is the *etymology*, which explains where the word came from. Toward the end of the *dash* entry, look at the part in brackets.

ME means Middle English, the English of around 1300 or 1400. The Middle English form of this word was pretty much the same as the form now.

The entry also tells us that the Middle English word for *dash* probably came from Old Norse (Norwegian), and we are asked to compare it (cf.) to a Danish and a Swedish word. These three are all Germanic languages.

English is a Germanic language, too, but with many words added from French and other languages. (Borrowing goes both ways; the French word for "beefsteak" is—*beefsteak*.)

The English language as you and I speak it is called *American English*. It differs in various ways from British English. For example, the spelling is sometimes different. Our word *labor* becomes the British *labour*, and we spell *civilization* with a *z*, but they spell it with an *s*.

Terminology also differs. We say *apartment*; they say *flat*. We say *sidewalk*; they say *pavement*. Our *elevator* becomes their *lift*; our word *subway* is their word *underground*; and the *hood* of a car is *bonnet* in British English. Can you think of other examples of what could be called Americanisms and Briticisms?

USING THE PRONUNCIATION KEY

Pronunciation keys vary somewhat from one dictionary to another, but basically they all work the same way. After the entry word, in parentheses, there is a phonetic spelling that tells how the word is pronounced. The phonetic spelling tells you not the letters that spell the word, but the sounds that make up the word.

The vowel sound in the word *brute*, for example, is shown as o͞o in the phonetic spelling:

brute (bro͞ot)

This is the sound o͞o as in the word *boot* according to the pronunciation key at the bottom of this page. Look down and find bo͞ot in the key.

This same sound is spelled with four letters (*ough*) in the word *through*:

through (thro͞o)

Four letters spell one sound, shown by the phonetic symbol o͞o.

All the words below have the o͞o sound in them. Listen:

boo   dew   sue   do   flu

No matter how the words are spelled, the phonetic symbol o͞o will be used for the vowel sound in all the words:

boo (bo͞o)   **dew** (do͞o)   **sue** (so͞o)   **do** (do͞o)   **flu** (flo͞o)

Now let's take the word *chair* and the phonetic spelling that follows it in a dictionary entry:

chair (châr)

First, take the ch in the phonetic spelling. This is the same sound as in *chief* in the pronunciation key. Look down and find chief. The next phonetic symbol is â. The key tells you that this sound is the same as the *a* sound in *dare*. Look down at *dâre* in the key. Last, the phonetic spelling shows an *r* sound. So *chair* rhymes with *dare*.

Now let's take a longer word, with three syllables (separated from each other in the dictionary entry by centered dots). Our word, *archaic*, is usually used to describe a word or custom that is no longer in general use. Here it is:

ar·cha·ic (är kā′ik)

The ä appears in *art* in the key below. The *ch* spelling is pronounced *k*, followed by the ā in *able* (see the key). This middle syllable, kā, rhymes with the word *day*. The slanting line after it (′) shows that it is the stressed syllable—it is spoken more loudly and with greater emphasis than the other syllables. The final syllable has the unmarked *i* of *if* in the key, plus a *k* sound.

Now say the word: archaic (är kā′ik). Archaic.

PRONUNCIATION KEY: *act, āble, dâre, ärt; ebb, ēqual; if, īce; hot, ōver, ôrder, oil, out; up, ûrge, ūse; bo͝ok, bo͞ot;* ə = *a* in *alone; sing; shoe; thin, that; chief; kept; go; just;* zh = *s* in *measure*

EXERCISE 3 Practicing with the Pronunciation Key

To learn the pronunciation of a new word, you must master the pronunciation key. The key gives the phonetic spelling, or "sound spelling," of the word. Remember, the letter *u* in the word *brute* is shown as the o͞o sound in bo͞ot in the phonetic spelling (bro͞ot).

Each word below has a letter or letters underlined, and the word's phonetic spelling is given in parentheses. Find the word in the key that tells the *sound* of the underlined letters, and write it next to the word. For an unmarked letter in the phonetic spelling, find the word in the key that has that letter without a mark. For example, the word *bread* (bred) has the vowel sound of the *e* in *ebb*. Here we go. The first answer is filled in for you.

1. b<u>oa</u>t (bōt)   ___ō̄ver___

2. b<u>ai</u>t (bāt)   _____

3. b<u>i</u>te (bīt)   _____

4. b<u>ea</u>t (bēt)   _____

5. b<u>i</u>t (bit)   _____

Next, try writing the phonetic, or sound, spelling of these words. Note that there may be more letters in a word than there are sounds. Try to *ignore the spelling; listen to the sounds* of the words.

6. right   would be   _____ _____ _____   (five letters but three sounds)

7. rule   would be   _____ _____ _____   (four letters but three sounds)

8. cent   would be   _____ _____ _____ _____   (four letters and four sounds)

9. seed   would be   _____ _____ _____   (four letters but three sounds)

10. cot   would be   _____ _____ _____   (three letters and three sounds)

Now check your work on this page.

1. ōver   2. āble   3. īce   4. ēqual   5. if   6. rīt   7. ro͞ol
8. sent   9. sēd   10. kot

Note that the letter *c* can represent an *s* sound, as in *cent*, or a *k* sound, as in *cot*. And remember that the *ch* spelling can represent the sound of *ch* in *chief*, as in *chair*, or the sound of *k* in *kept*, as in *archaic*.

And different spellings can represent the same sound, as we saw with *dew*, *do*, and *due*.

WORDS ARE SOUNDS—OR COMBINATIONS OF SOUNDS

Spelling

You can't tell by its spelling what a word sounds like. These three sets don't look alike:

so/sew two/too/to rain/rein

But they sound alike.

And these three sets do look alike:

new/sew paid/said bough/tough/through

But they don't sound alike.

English can be tricky that way. Sound and spelling can fool you. For example, some words that rhyme with *graph* are *calf*, *giraffe*, and *laugh*. The *ch* in *archbishop* has the sound of *ch* in *chief*. But in *architect* it has the sound of *k* in *kept*.

And look at the double *c* in *occur* and *accident*. The *cc* in *occur* has only the sound of *k* in *kept*. But in *accident* the *cc* has first a *k* sound and then an *s* sound in the phonetic spelling (ak′si dent).

The moral of this story is: you can't tell the sound by the spelling. You need the phonetic spelling and the pronunciation key!

Stress or Accent

Dictionaries show two kinds of stress: a minor one, with a light stress mark (′), and a main stress, with a darker stress mark (′). Listen to these familiar three-syllable words, *afternoon* and *entertain*:

af′ter noon′ en′ter tain′

As the words get longer, it becomes more important to recognize the main stress as well as the sound of the stressed syllable. As an example, let's take two fairly short words, *personal* and *personnel*. (*Personnel* means the people working in an organization, as "office personnel.") Check the pronunciation against the key at the bottom of the page. Note the main stresses.

personal (pûr′sə nəl) **personnel** (pûr′sə nel′)

Say the two words to yourself. Hear the difference. The syllables that get the main stress are important, aren't they?

As you work the exercise on the opposite page, use the pronunciation key below.

PRONUNCIATION KEY: act, āble, dâre, ärt; ebb, ēqual; if, īce; hot, ōver, ôrder, oil, out; up, ûrge, ūse; book, boot; ə = a in *alone*; sing; shoe; thin, that; chief; kept; go; just; zh = s in *measure*

EXERCISE 4   Finding the Main Stress, or Accent

Let's start with some three-syllable words. Here's one: *archetype*.

1. **ar·che·type** (är′ki tīp′), *n.*   the first form or first example of something.
   The word in the pronunciation key that explains the *a* sound in the stressed
   syllable is the fourth word, the one with two dots (called a dieresis) over the letter *a*.

   This is the word _____
   The *ch* has a *k* sound, as in *kept*.
   Read this sentence: *The English House of Commons was the archetype of our House
   of Representatives.*

2. **An·tie·tam** (an tē′təm), *n.*, cap. (capitalized)   place of a Civil War battle.
   The word in the key that explains the sound of the *ie* in the stressed syllable

   is _____
   Say the word to yourself, stressing the middle syllable: An*tie*tam. Then read this
   sentence: *The military situation changed after the battle of Antietam.*

3. Here are five-syllable words. You know the meanings. After each one, write the
   word from the key that explains the sound of the vowel in the syllable that gets
   the *main* stress.

   dis·crim·i·na·tion (di skrim′ə nā′shən)   _____

   dis·hon·or·a·ble (dis on′ər ə bəl)   _____

4. Let's try one unfamiliar six-syllable word.

   an·te·di·lu·vi·an (an′tē di lōō′vē ən), *adj.*   very old, esp. before the Flood.
   The word is often used humorously, to suggest that something seems so old it might
   have come from before the Flood described in the Bible, as in this remark: *What
   an antediluvian idea!*

5. You know these words. Both the meaning and the sound are familiar. Match each
   one with the word from the key that explains the sound of the underlined letter
   or letters.

   A. l<u>oo</u>k (lŏŏk)   _____   C. c<u>a</u>t (kat)   _____

   B. c<u>o</u>ld (kōld)   _____   D. c<u>o</u>rn (kôrn)   _____

   Do you notice that all three words with the letter *c* have a *k* sound?
   In *cent*, the letter *c* has an *s* sound, doesn't it?

Putting together in your mind the *look* and the *sound* of a word—its pronunciation—
along with its *meaning*, is the way to master that word.

A SAMPLE DICTIONARY PAGE

enterostomy   **e.o.**

en·ter·os·to·my (en′tə ros′tə mē), *n.   Surg.* the making of an artificial opening into the small intestine.

en·ter·o·tox·e·mi·a (en′ tə rō tok sē′mē ə), n.   *Vet. Sci.* a disease of sheep caused by severe poisoning in the intestinal tract.

en·thet·ic (en thet′ik), *adj.*   introduced from without, as disease caused by inoculation.

en·thrall (en thrôl′), *v.t.*   **1.** to captivate, charm.   **2.** to put or hold in thralldom; subjugate. Also, **inthrall, inthral.   —enthraller,** *n.*   **—enthrallment,** *n.*

en·thuse (en thōōz′), *U.S. Colloq. v.i.*   **1.** to become enthusiastic; to show enthusiasm. *v.t.* **2.** to move to enthusiasm. [back formation from ENTHUSIASM]

en·tice (en tīs′), *v.t.*   to draw on by exciting hope or desire; allure. [ME *entyce,* t. OF *enticier,* incite]

en·tire·ty (en tīər′tē), *n., pl.,* **-ties** (-tēz).   **1.** state of being entire; completeness.   **2.** that which is entire; the whole.

en·ti·tle (en tīt′əl), *v.t.*   **1.** to give a person or thing a title, right, or claim to something.   **2.** to call by a particular title or name.   **3.** to designate a person by an honorary title. Also, **intitle.** [ME *entitle,* t. OF *entituler* t. LL *intitulare*]

en·ti·ty (en′ti tē) *n., pl.* **-ties** (-tēz).   **1.** something that has a real existence.   **2.** being or existence.   **3.** essential nature. [t. LL *entitas*]

entom., entomology. Also, **entomol.**

en·tomb (en tōōm′), *v.t.*   **1.** to place in a tomb.   **2.** to serve as a tomb for. Also, **intomb.** [t. OF *entomber*]   **—entombment,** *n.*

entomo-, a word element meaning insect. Also, before vowels, **entom-.**

en·to·mol·o·gize (en′tə mol′ə jīz′), *v.i.*   **1.** to study entomology.   **2.** to gather entomological specimens.

en·to·mol·o·gy (en′tə mol′ə jē), *n.* the branch of zoology that treats of insects.   **—entomological,** *adj.*   **—entomologist,** *n.*

en·train (en trān′), *v.i., v.t.*   to put or go aboard a train.   **—entrainment,** *n.*

en·trance (en′trəns), *n.*   **1.** act of entering, as into a place.   **2.** a point or place of entering; an opening or passage for entering.   **3.** power or liberty of entering; admission.   **4.** *Theat.* the moment, or place in the script, when an actor comes on to the stage. [t. OF *entrer*]   **—Syn. 1.** entry, ingress.

en·trant (en′trənt), *n.*   **1.** one who enters.   **2.** a new member, as of an association.   **3.** a competitor in a contest.

en·treas·ure (en trezh′ər), *v.t.* to lay up in or as in a treasury.

en·tre·côte (än trə kōt′), *n. French*   rib steak.

e.o., *ex officio,* through the power of one's position or office.

EXERCISE 5   Working with a Dictionary Page

Use the sample dictionary page opposite to answer these.

1. Which definition of *entitle* would best fit this sentence?
    *Being my uncle doesn't entitle you to lecture me this
    way!*   Number _____

2. Look at the entry for the word *entrecôte*. (It's the
    next to the last word.) Check the pronunciation
    carefully. The best rhyme word for this would be one
    of the following:
    A. but   B. beat   C. boat   D. lot   E. boot   Which one? _____

3. Look at the entry for the word *entity*. There is a
    plural ending given for this noun. Say the plural form
    to yourself. The plural of *entity* would rhyme with one
    of these words:
    A. cries   B. breeze   C. geese   D. kiss   Which one? _____

4. The word element *entomo-*, which is shown, means insect.
    How many words are given in which this word element appears?   _____

5. A word meaning *one who studies insects* is
    shown in one of the entries. What word is it?   _____

6. Which word in the pronunciation key
    explains the sound for the letter *s* in
    entreasure? (The answer is a word.)   _____

7. In what special field is the word
    enterostomy used?   _____

8. In what special field is the word *entrance*
    used with the meaning it has in this
    sentence? *Hamlet's entrance comes early in
    the first scene of the play.*
       Your answer will be the name of the
    special field.   _____

9. All the standard abbreviations are listed in a college dictionary. Explain the
    meaning of the abbreviation used in this sentence. *His uncle the Mayor was able to*

    help him, e.o., that is. _____

Why are *enterostomy* and *e.o.* shown at the top of the opposite page? Because they
are the first and last words listed on that particular page. They are called guide-
words or catchwords.

EXERCISE 6   Working with Pronunciation: The Main Stress

Here are entries for the words you'll work with in this exercise.

an·tiph·o·nal (an tif′ə nəl), *adj.* having to do with a verse or song to be sung in
 alternate parts.
im·pi·ous (im′pē əs), *adj.* not pious; disrespectful.
in·cho·ate (in kō′it), *adj.* not complete; not well formed or organized.
mag·na·nim·i·ty (mag′nə nim′i tē), *n.* generosity; freedom from malice;
 high-mindedness.
te·lep·a·thy (tə lep′ə thē), *n.* communication between minds by some means other
 than sensory perception.

1. We all enjoy *antiphonal* singing.
    A. Underline the syllable that receives the main stress. This is
       syllable number   _____
    B. What word in the key at the bottom of this page tells the sound of
       the vowel in the syllable that gets the main stress?   _____

    C. What word in the key explains the sound of the third syllable?   _____
    D. Check the meaning of the word and keep this in mind as you say
       the word to yourself. Read the sentence given, for practice.

2. That was an *impious* remark!
    A. This word has three syllables. Underline the stressed syllable.
       This is syllable number   _____
    B. Read the sentence given, for practice. Keep in mind the meaning
       of the word *impious* as you say it.

3. The general's plans are still *inchoate* at this time.
    A. Give the number of the stressed syllable.   _____
    B. Does the *ch* in this word have the sound of *ch* in *chief* or the sound
       of *k* in *kept*?   _____
    C. The word in the key that explains the sound of the letter *o* in the
       stressed syllable is the word   _____

4. His *magnanimity* astonished and pleased us.
   A. This is a longer word. Remember that the centered dots in an entry word mark the syllables. How many syllables does this word have? _____
   B. Underline the syllable that receives the main stress. What word is given in the key to explain the sound of the vowel in this syllable? _____
   C. Carefully check the pronunciation of the word. Now read the sentence given, keeping the meaning of *magnanimity* in mind as you say the word. _____

5. Have you ever tried to communicate with someone by *telepathy*?
   A. Underline the syllable that receives the stress. Give the number of this syllable. _____
   B. What word does the key give to explain the sound of the vowel in this syllable? _____
   C. Have you ever heard stories of people communicating by telepathy? It's an interesting word, expressing an interesting idea. Read the sentence given above, keeping the meaning of *telepathy* in mind as you do so. _____

As you read, and particularly as you study, you need to understand the words that are important in the passage you're reading. And, as mentioned before, mastery of a word always includes knowing how to pronounce it.

   Now, write two sentences of your own, using in each sentence one of the words you have worked with in this exercise. Take two words that you feel fairly sure of.

6. _____

   _____

7. _____

   _____

Go back to your sentences and underline the words you selected. Be sure you have used them right.

EXERCISE 7   Practice with Pronunciation

There are certain simple, everyday words that have two pronunciations, both given in the dictionary. Both are correct.

For each word below, write next to it the word from the key showing the sound of the vowel—the vowel in the *stressed* syllable for the words of more than one syllable —for the first pronunciation and then for the second pronunciation.

	First	*Word from key*	*Second*	*Word from key*
1. tomato	(tə mā′tō)	_____	(tə mä′tō)	_____
2. creek	(krēk)	_____	(krik)	_____
3. either	(ē′thər)	_____	(i′thər)	_____
4. aunt	(ant)	_____	(änt)	_____
5. drama	(drä′mə)	_____	(dram′ə)	_____

6. Say each word both ways. Hear how different the word sounds as you go from one pronunciation to the other. Which pronunciation do *you* use? Both are correct. Go back and circle the phonetic spelling for the pronunciation that you use: for example, circle (krēk) if you say that, or (krik) if you use that pronunciation.

   Usually, in a college class, some people use one pronunciation, some the other, because of different backgrounds. For example, if you're not from Chicago, you may use the pronunciation (shi kä′gō), but if you go there you'll hear (shi kô′gō). That's the way Chicagoans say it.

7. Occasionally, the pronunciation of a single letter or group of letters is the key to the pronunciation of a word. The letter or letters underlined in the following words are important in the pronunciation of the words.
   A. **heinous** (hā′nəs), *adj.* hateful, abominable.
      Now for the word from the key to explain the sound of the *ei*. _____

      The newspapers did not report that heinous crime. As you say the sentence to yourself, carefully pronounce the word *heinous.* Hear the sound of the *a* in *able?* Heinous—a heinous crime.

   B. **archives** (är′kīvz), *n.* records, or the place where they are stored.

      The *ch* sound is explained in the pronunciation key by the word _____

      And the *i* in the second syllable has the sound of the *i* in the word _____

      To look up that date, we'll have to go back to the archives. Say the sentence to yourself. Pronounce the word *archives.*

PRONUNCIATION KEY: *a*ct, *ā*ble, d*â*re, *ä*rt; *e*bb, *ē*qual; *i*f, *ī*ce; h*o*t, *ō*ver, *ô*rder, *oi*l, *ou*t; *u*p, *û*rge, *ū*se; b*oo*k, b*oo*t; ə = *a* in alone; si*ng*; *sh*oe; *th*in, *th*at; *ch*ief; kept; go; just; *zh* = *s* in *measure*

8. **antip͟asto** (än′tē päs′tô), *n.* an assortment of appetizers (Italian cookery).
   Because this word comes to us from the Italian, the sound of the *a* in the stressed syllable is different from what it would be for a similar word in American English.
   The word in the key that explains the sound of this *a* is the word _____

   Say the word to yourself first: *antipasto*. Now read the sentence; pronounce the word. *For lunch we ordered just coffee and an antipasto.*

9. **sl͟e͟ight** (slīt), *n.* sleight of hand; skill with hands, as in juggling.

   The word in the key for the *ei* spelling here is the word _____

   Say the word; pronounce it as you read the sentence. *As he pulled the rabbit from his hat, we admired his sleight of hand.*

   > Heinous has an *ei* with the sound of *a* in *able*.
   > Sleight has an *ei* with the sound of *i* in *ice*.

   Review: say the two words—*heinous, sleight.*

10. **comfortable** (kum′fər tə bəl), *adj.* You know the meaning.
    In the usual pronunciation, there are three syllables in which the vowel letters have the sound represented by the symbol ə (called the schwa). The explanation

    of this sound given in the key is the word _____
    The word *comfortable* can also be pronounced with three syllables: kumf′tə bəl.

    In the following words, all of which you know, the second vowel has the schwa sound. Underline the vowel in the second syllable of each word. Listen to the sound, which is the same for all of the underlined vowels.

    pencil   circus   panel   mirror   final

    The spelling varies: *i, u, e, o,* and *a.* But the sound is the same: the sound of *a* in *alone.* This is one of the most common vowel sounds in English.

Remember that the important words for *you* to learn—both meaning and sound—are the *idea words,* or *concept words,* in the courses you are taking in college.

WORD STUDY

What's an *eskimologist*?

(The main stress here is on the third syllable—eski*mo*logist, with a short *o*, as in *hot*.)

Let's start with *eskimo*, or *Eskimo*, the name of a people of the far north.

Then we need the root *-logy*, meaning the study of something. We see this root in words like *psychology* and *sociology*.

Next comes the suffix *-ist*, which signifies a person who does something, as in *artist*, *dentist*, or *psychologist*.

When we put these together, we have *eskimologist*. This person, this eskimologist, is someone who studies the culture and language of the eskimos.

Try saying the word to yourself: eski*mo*logist.

Suppose you meet a man who's famous for *prestidigitation*. What's that?

(The main stress here is on the *ta* syllable, with a long *a*, as in *able*.)

First, take *presto*, meaning fast or lively. Add *digit*, which here means finger. Then finish off with *-ation*, meaning the act or process of.

The man you met was famous for juggling or sleight of hand of some kind. Maybe he could pull a rabbit out of a hat.

Practice saying this word, being sure to get in all the syllables. There are six.

The man you met was famous for prestidigi*ta*tion.

Now let's reverse the process. Let's begin with *establish* and then move on to *establishment*, an existing order or system.

England has an "established," or official church, the Anglo-Catholic church.

An *establishmentarian* is a person who is in favor of having an established church, who likes the system.

Establishmentarianism is the word for the system. (The stress here is on the *tar* syllable, which rhymes with *dare*.)

On the other hand, a *dis*establishmentarian is a person who does *not* like having an established church. *Disestablishmentarianism* is what this belief is called. A person who believes in it opposes the idea of having an established church.

At one time in England there was a very strong movement for disestablishment. Disestablishmentarianism became stronger and stronger. (When you say that long word, the stress is still on *tar*.)

The people who liked having an established, or official, church became alarmed. They started a movement called

<u>anti</u>disestablishmentarianism.

WORD ELEMENTS

We're all aware of the meaning of some word elements. If we say someone is *supersensitive* or *supersilly*, the prefix *super-* is familiar and always means the same thing, so anyone will know what those words mean.

But not all word elements are so obliging, some have two or three meanings. For example, *-graph* can mean either "picture" or "writing." In the words *photograph* and *biography*, we see the two meanings at work. *Photo-* and *bio-* are more reliable. The first always means "light" and the second always means "life". (A photograph is a picture made with light; a biography is the written account of a life.)

Below we have a list of some common word elements. We have word bases such as *lith-*, prefixes such as *sub-*, and suffixes such as *-ism*. You'll use this list as you do the word work on the following pages.

ambi-, both, on both sides
auto-, self, same
bio-, life
-chrome, color
chron-, time
circum-, around
-en, as a verb suffix, to make; also, to become
eu-, good, well
gene, from a Greek word meaning breed or kind
-graph, picture or writing
hetero-, different
-ish, resembling; also, somewhat
-ism, a set of ideas or doctrines; also, action or practice
-ize, to make; also, to become
lith-, stone
-logy, knowledge or study of; also, science of
magn-, great, large

meta-, along with, after; often meaning change
mono-, one
morph-, form
novus (Latin), new
-osis, act or process; also, state or condition
patho-, feeling or suffering; disease
phone (or **phon-**), sound
poly-, many
psych-, **psycho-**, spirit or mind
re-, again; also, back
sub-, under
sym-, variant form of **syn-**
syn-, together
terra (Latin), earth, land
theo-, pertaining to the gods
therap-, pertaining to treatment or cure
therm-, pertaining to heat

These word elements and many more will be listed in any good college-level dictionary. As you go on in college, you'll gradually acquire knowledge of many of them, which will help you to learn, and to remember, the vocabulary you need for your courses.

EXERCISE 8   Working with Word Elements

Each of the following sentences contains one word that may be unfamiliar to you. Check the pronunciation, using the pronunciation key below, and the meaning, using *the context of the sentence* as one way to find meaning and also using, if necessary, the list of word elements on the opposite page.

1. **polychromatic** (pol′ē krō mat′ik).   The painting he produced was a huge polychromatic design, dazzling in its array of colors.

   Polychromatic means _____

2. **euphonious** (ū fō′nē əs)   The girl who sang for us had a most euphonious voice, and she was well received by the audience.

   Euphonious means _____

3. **heterogeneous** (het′ər ə jē′nē əs)   We were a truly heterogeneous group; no two felt or thought alike, because of our different backgrounds.

   Heterogeneous means _____

4. **subterranean** (sub′tə rā′nē ən)   Subterranean deposits of the precious metal had lain unsuspected beneath our cornfields for all those years.

   Subterranean means _____

5. **renovate** (ren′ə vāt′)   The Smiths decided to buy an old house and renovate it, since it had historical value and was worth working on.

   Renovate means _____

Read aloud the sentences given, for practice with both meaning and pronunciation. Hear the word; think about the meaning. Now choose two of the words you have just worked with and use them in sentences of your own. Underline the word as it appears in your sentence.

6. _____

   _____

7. _____

   _____

PRONUNCIATION KEY: a*ct*, ā*ble*, d*âre*, ä*rt*; e*bb*, ē*qual*; *if*, ī*ce*; *hot*, ō*ver*, ô*rder*, *oil*, *out*; *up*, û*rge*, ū*se*; bo͝o*k*, bo͞o*t*; ə = *a* in *alone*; *sin͡g*; *shoe*; *thin*, *that*; *chief*; *kept*; *go*; *just*; zh = *s* in *measure*

EXERCISE 9   Selecting Definitions of Word Bases or Elements

Many word elements or bases, like *-graph* and *photo-*, appear over and over in English. Find, on page 152, the meaning of the underlined part of each word below, and write down *the one definition that fits the word* in which the part appears. Remember, you are not defining the whole word—just the underlined element.

1. *auto<u>graph</u>*   Scott has the autograph of a famous movie star.

   _____

2. *<u>therm</u>al*   Deer hunters often wear thermal underwear in cold weather.

   _____

3. *<u>thera</u>pist*   After a long period of suffering, I went to a therapist.

   _____

4. *syn<u>chron</u>ize*   To carry out our plan, we had to synchronize our watches.

   _____

5. *<u>photo</u>synthesis*   Photosynthesis is the way plants synthesize, or manufacture, food.

   _____

6. *mono<u>lith</u>*   The threshold of the building was one huge monolith.

   _____

7. *<u>bio</u>tic*   In a biotic colony, more than one species live together.

   _____

8. *<u>theo</u>logy*   Since she liked the study of theology, she became a minister.

   _____

9. *<u>mag</u>nify*   I had to magnify the tiny print in order to be able to read it.

   _____

10. *meta<u>morph</u>osis*   When a caterpillar becomes a butterfly, we have an example of metamorphosis.

    _____

EXERCISE 10   Defining the Whole Word

The *context* of a sentence or a passage helps us to understand word meanings. To understand the meanings of the words in the exercise on page 154, reread each sentence. Then, if necessary, look up on page 152 the meaning of another key part of the word—for example, *syn-* in *synchronize* or *meta-* in *metamorphosis*. If this is still not enough, check the word in your dictionary.

Now write a simple definition of the word as it is used in the sentence on page 154.

1. autograph _____

2. thermal _____

3. therapist _____

4. synchronize _____

5. photosynthesis _____

6. monolith _____

7. biotic _____

8. theology _____

9. magnify _____

10. metamorphosis _____

Again, choose two of the words you have worked with here and use them in sentences of your own. Choose words you want to master.

11. _____

_____

12. _____

_____

Read your sentences aloud. Hear the word; think of the meaning. Have you added these words to your vocabulary?

The main purpose of this word study section, however, is not primarily to improve your vocabulary. The main purpose is to show you that many of the complex words you encounter in college are easier to master if you know the pronunciation and if you know the meaning of a key word element.

EXERCISE 11   Working with Prefixes and Suffixes

Prefixes and suffixes have meanings in themselves, which affect the meaning of the words they are part of. Look up, on page 152, the underlined part of each word here—prefix or suffix. Remember you're not looking up the whole word, but just the prefix or suffix.

Be sure you take *the definition that is appropriate for the word* in which the prefix or suffix appears. In *legalize*, for example, *-ize* can mean "to make" or it can mean "to become." Which meaning is appropriate?

1. *legalize*   Should a law be passed to legalize this drug?

   _____

2. *sympathetic*   Don't you feel sympathetic toward the poor fellow?

   _____

3. *psychology*   Studying psychology helps you to understand people.

   _____

4. *pinkish*   Her dress was pinkish, with white trim. (Choose carefully.)

   _____

5. *boyish*   My uncle Joe, who's forty, still has a boyish look.

   _____

6. *ambiguous*   The meaning of the passage was ambiguous; I just couldn't tell.

   _____

7. *circumvent*   I don't want to get into trouble; instead, I'll circumvent the rule.

   _____

8. *socialism*   National ownership of the means of production is called socialism.

   _____

9. *sweeten*   She used three teaspoonfuls of sugar to sweeten her tea.

   _____

10. *subhuman*   In that costume, Jerry, you look positively subhuman.

   _____

EXERCISE 12 Prefixes and Suffixes: The Whole Word

The sentences on page 156 probably helped you to understand the meaning of the whole word—such as *legalize*. Remember the list of word elements, prefixes, and suffixes on page 152. You may want to look up *path-* to define *sympathetic*, or *psycho-* for *psychology*. And there's always the dictionary.

Write a *simple* definition of each word as it is used in the sentences on page 156.

1. legalize _____

2. sympathetic _____

3. psychology _____

4. pinkish _____

5. boyish _____

6. ambiguous _____

7. circumvent _____

8. socialism _____

9. sweeten _____

10. subhuman _____

Choose two words from this list to use in sentences of your own. Don't take an easy one, such as *sweeten*. Instead, choose a word you want to learn.

11. _____

_____

12. _____

_____

Do you remember what the purpose of this section of the book is? It is to show you that many of the concept words you need to know for your college work will be easier to learn if you know the meaning of key word parts. Some word elements, such as *bi-*, *tri-*, and *cycle*, you already know. You know the difference between a bicycle and a tricycle. And then there's the *uni*cycle—it has only *one* wheel.

WORD ANALYSIS

Study this analysis of the word *anthropomorphic*.

1. Word and part of speech: *anthropomorphic*, adjective

2. Syllabication and pronunciation: an·thro·po·mor·phic (an′thrə pə môr′fik).

   Practice saying the word: *anthropomorphic*.

3. Division of the word into meaningful word elements: *anthropo / morph / ic*

   anthropo-, man
   morph-, form
   -ic, resembling

4. Present meaning of *anthropomorphic*: attributing human qualities to animals, objects, or gods

5. Words with the root *morph* in common:

   morphology, the study of form
   metamorphosis, the act of changing form
   amorphous, lacking form

   Words with the root *anthropo* in common:

   anthropology, the study of man
   anthropoid, resembling man (said of an ape)
   anthropophagi, cannibals (eaters of men)

6. Use in a sentence:

   Many religions have an anthropomorphic concept or vision of their god.

   Read the sentence aloud. Hear the sound; think of the meaning.

EXERCISE 13   Practicing Word Analysis

Choose one of these words to analyze, following the model given on page 158:

> automotive, benefactor, bilingual, cryptogram, decapitate, desalinization, egocentric, eradicate, homogeneous, illegible, implacable, improvident, interventionist, intramural, invocation, irrevocable, isocracy, omniscient, pedometer, polyandry, progenitor, reconstitute, renovation, subaqueous, subcutaneous, unremitting

You'll need a good dictionary. If necessary, go to your library and ask to use one of the college dictionaries. Also, if you're stuck, you can ask the reference librarian to help you.

1. Word and part of speech: _____

2. Syllabication and pronunciation: _____

   Practice saying the word. Refer to the key at the bottom of page 158.

3. Division of the word into meaningful word elements: _____
   (List the elements and their meanings in this space.)

   _____

   _____

   _____

4. Present meaning of the word: _____

5. Words with the root _____ in common:

   _____

   _____

   Words with the root _____ in common:

   _____

   _____

6. Use in a sentence:

   _____

   Read the sentence aloud. Hear the sound of the word; think of the meaning.

NAMES AND SPECIAL REFERENCES

To understand your college textbooks, you sometimes need to look up words, like *metamorphosis* or *photosynthesis*. These are concept or idea words in a particular subject, and they're very important for you to master if you want to do well in that subject.

There also are many special references and terms. Suppose you come across the name *Demosthenes* (di mos′thə nēz). Your college dictionary will tell you that he was a Greek politician and orator of the fourth century B.C. And probably that's all you need to know. Or take the word *Deuteronomy* (dōō′ tə ron′ə mē).

In the case of such special words, what you're usually trying to do is *to identify the reference* without getting a lot of unnecessary information.

This is not always easy. And sometimes you *need* to know more about a special term. *You* must be the judge of how much you need to know.

Let's go back to *Deuteronomy*. It is the fifth book of the Old Testament in the Bible.

Is that all you need to know? Or do you need to know also that this is the last of the five books of the Torah, or Law? That this book is a code of civil and religious laws and that it recounts Moses' advice to the Israelites shortly before his death? That it is important in Hebrew-Jewish history and is frequently quoted in the New Testament?

The *Encyclopaedia Britannica* gives you two closely printed pages of details about this important Old Testament book. A good college-level dictionary will give you only the basic identification.

In addition to references to famous people, places, and documents, there are many other kinds of words and terms that need attention.

For example, there are the special terms used on examinations, which we studied in chapter 1; connectors, like *moreover* and *nonetheless*; qualifiers, such as *rarely* and *occasionally*; words that are look-alikes, such as *personal* and *personnel*; and words occurring in college catalogues.

We'll practice with all these kinds of words, then work with words in context, and finally go on to some more word study and dictionary review.

EXERCISE 14   Using the Dictionary for Special References

As we read, we often find names, special terms, or references that we're not familiar with. We may not need to know very much about them—usually just their basic significance in the passage. After consulting a good college-level dictionary, define or identify the underlined names or terms in the sentences below. Write down *enough to identify the term*, but *no more than necessary*.

1. For that information, you'll have to consult the <u>Library of Congress</u>.

   The Library of Congress is _____

2. He was quoting <u>James Madison</u> on the need for a strong executive.

   James Madison was _____

3. Those old-timers were interested in just one thing: maintaining the <u>status quo</u>.

   The status quo is _____

4. The old man has retired and is living on <u>social security</u> and his savings.

   Here, the term social security means _____

5. <u>New Orleans</u> was the economic center of this entire area.

   New Orleans is _____

6. The name <u>Miltiades</u> became a watchword, a symbol of the fight for freedom.

   Miltiades was _____

   _____

If you are studying Greek history, you will need to know quite a bit about Miltiades. Otherwise, you need only identify him briefly.

CONNECTING WORDS: CONJUNCTIONS OR CONNECTORS

Research in reading has shown that the understanding of conjunctions and connectors is of particular importance in reading comprehension.

Here is a listing of eight kinds of meaning that common English connectors can express, with several examples of each kind. Read the list slowly, noting the examples of each kind of meaning.

addition and, also, too, moreover, furthermore, in addition, another, more, besides
contrast but, yet, still, however, nevertheless, on the other hand, nonetheless
alternation or, or else, otherwise, if not . . . then, either . . .or, neither . . . nor
cause and effect so, therefore, consequently, hence, as a result, since, because, thus, accordingly, for, for this reason
condition if, although, even though, provided that, unless, whether or not, in case
time later, then, while, as, after, meanwhile, earlier, soon, subsequently, when
space nearby, here, across from, there, above, around, farther on, wherever, beyond, below, in back of
reference this, that, these, those, such, both

Other kinds of references include the repetition of nouns and the use of pronouns for nouns, as well as the use of paraphrase: John . . . he . . . this man . . . the hero . . . John . . .

Connectors with various meanings, like *as a result* or *later* or *even though* or *that*, can provide transitions between what has gone before and what lies ahead.

In these sentences we look first backward and then forward.

This caused more trouble.

And so I told him another lie.

In the sentences below, mark with arrows all words and expressions that refer backward or forward.

After this event, we left quietly.

Consequently, we had to dream up another plan.

Nevertheless, the old fool refused.

In this way, there began a new era.

If he comes, I'll give him some additional help.

EXERCISE 15   Connectors That Fit the Sentence

The meaning of a connector is an important part of the meaning of the sentence in which it is used. In each of the sentences marked A, choose one of these connectors to fit the meaning of the sentence: *otherwise, however, moreover, nevertheless, furthermore, consequently, therefore, subsequently.*

In each sentence marked B, use the list on page 162 to select a connector from the group indicated: *contrast, condition, alternation, cause and effect,* etc. Be sure to choose one that fits the meaning of the sentence.

1. A. Bert doesn't have an idea in his head; _____ he's a
       (Contrast)
    charming fellow.

   B. _____ Bert doesn't have an idea in his head, he's a
      (Condition)
    charming fellow.

2. A. The President has vetoed the bill; _____ it will be returned
       (Cause and Effect)
    to Congress.

   B. _____ the President has vetoed the bill, it will be returned
      (Cause and Effect)
    to Congress.

3. A. You'll just have to start getting to work on time; _____
       (Alternation)
    the boss will surely fire you.

   B. _____ you don't start getting to work on time, the boss
      (Condition)
    will surely fire you.

4. A. Percy has confessed publicly that he committed the crime; _____
       (Addition)
    he has put his confession in writing.

   B. _____ confessing publicly that he committed the crime,
      (Addition)
    Percy has put his confession in writing.

Notice how the change of a connector can change the meaning of a sentence.

> *Although* Ed's going to Alaska, I'm planning to go there myself.
> *Since* Ed's going to Alaska, I'm planning to go there myself.
> *Whether or not* Ed's going to Alaska, I'm planning to go there myself.
> *In addition to* Ed's going to Alaska, I'm planning to go there myself.
> *Either* Ed's going to Alaska *or* I'm planning to go there myself.

Which sentences suggest that both Ed and I are going? Which that only one of us will go?

QUALIFYING WORDS

Sometimes a word like *never* or *seldom*—or the lack of such a word—is the one thing that makes a statement true or false. These are *qualifying words*.

EXERCISE 16   Analyzing Qualifying Words

Mark each one of these statements T, for true, or F, for false. If you find some statements that have no clear answer, mark them with a question mark.

1. Women are *always* better drivers than men. _____

2. Evidence from a lie detector is *never* considered evidence of guilt. _____

3. Evidence from a lie detector is *sometimes* considered helpful. _____

4. Needles are *always* used for sewing purposes. _____

5. A messenger from the enemy is *invariably* sent to request a truce. _____

6. Used cars are *rarely* purchased by people who cannot afford them. _____

7. *All* doctors are concerned about reasonable fees. _____

8. *Occasionally* shy people enjoy public speaking. _____

9. An electric clock *inevitably* tells the correct time. _____

10. Drivers who are not accident-prone *probably* have fewer accidents than those who are. _____

11. *Occasionally* a niece is older than her aunt. _____

12. The son of your mother's older sister is *sometimes* your cousin. _____

13. A brick *usually* has six sides. _____

14. Small errors may *sometimes* prove to be of great consequence. _____

For any three of the statements that you marked F, give a different qualifying word that makes the statement true. In statement 1, for example, you could say *sometimes*: Women are *sometimes* better drivers than men.

15. No. _____ qualifying word _____

16. No. _____ qualifying word _____

17. No. _____ qualifying word _____

EXERCISE 17　Distinguishing Between Words That Look Alike

Some pairs of words look alike. Generally, we don't confuse them when we speak. But in reading we may fail to distinguish between them.

Take a close look at the italicized words in these sentences.

1. One of the office *personnel* has a *personal* problem he wants to talk to you about. Which of the two words means the people employed somewhere?

   _____
   　　(Write clearly)

2. Let's *proceed* with our business. Please *precede* me into the conference room.

   Which word means to go before? _____

3. His *affection* for you was very real. His pretended respect for your father, however, was merely an *affectation*.

   Which word means a pretense? _____

4. You may *persecute* him with jokes and sarcasm, but you can't *prosecute* him.

   Which word means to take legal action against someone? _____

5. Tony was really *stimulated* by the wine, but Al was *simulating* drunkenness.

   Which word means pretending? _____

6. Your *illegible* handwriting will make you *ineligible* for this job.

   Which word means not readable? _____

   Which word means not acceptable? _____

7. His *martial* accomplishments as a young man were notable; so were his *marital* failures later in life.

   Which word refers to war? _____

   Which to marriage? _____

8. He's a *hypocritical* person, all right, and not nearly as virtuous as he wants us to think. Still, I think you're *hypercritical*—you judge him too harshly.

   Which word means too critical? _____

   Which one means full of pretense? _____

WORDS FROM A COLLEGE CATALOGUE

In order to understand many college procedures, you need to know the special terminology used in college catalogues. The terms vary only slightly from one college to another, even though the actual requirements and regulations of colleges differ quite a bit.

By reading the catalogue of the college you are attending or that of a college you are thinking of attending, you should be able to find the answers to such questions as the following. To understand the questions, you must understand the italicized terms.

1. Is the college *accredited* by a regional accrediting association, such as the North Central Association or the Middle States Association? If not, your credits may not be accepted by another college.

2. Are there *counselors* available to advise you before you enter the college?

3. Are there special requirements for the *curriculum* you're interested in?

4. How many *required courses* and how many *electives* are there in the curriculum?

5. What's the difference between a two-year *vocational* curriculum and *transfer* courses?

6. Are you likely to be required to take *remedial* reading, writing, or math?

7. Does the college have a clear *attendance policy*?

8. If there's one course you especially want to take, is there a *prerequisite* for that course?

9. Are you allowed to *audit* a course without paying tuition? Under what conditions is a student allowed to *audit*?

10. Does the college have good *audio-visual* services?

11. How long can you keep a library book that you've checked out at the *circulation* desk?

12. Where do you find the *reference librarian*?

13. When might you consult the *dean of instruction* or a *department chairperson*?

14. When might you consult the *dean of students*?

15. When you leave the college, under what conditions will the *registrar* give you a *transcript* of your record?

Your college catalogue can give you reliable answers to these and other questions. Read the catalogue! If there's something in it you don't understand, consult a college counselor.

EXERCISE 18 Defining Words from a College Catalogue

Your college catalogue is a valuable reference work for you as a student. The words from it used on the previous page represent many important aspects of college life.

In the spaces provided below, explain as clearly as you can the meaning of any of these words you don't thoroughly understand. Any college dictionary will help you. Or you might want to consult a counselor or other college official.

_____

_____

_____

_____

_____

_____

_____

_____

_____

REVIEW: WORD STUDY

Words are things we can't live without. As children, we learn them by hearing them. And we continue to learn them this way, as well as in other ways. Knowing the sound of a word is basic to the mastery of that word.

We've seen that words with different spellings can sound alike.

do/due/dew   so/sew   no/know   dough/doe   ruff/rough

But some words work the other way—they are spelled the same, but they are pronounced differently.

Jim, will you *row* the boat?   Let's not get into a *row*.

You're *close* enough.   Please *close* the door.

Sometimes the stress, or accent, shifts according to how the word is used.

Our ideas *conflict*.   Let's avoid physical *conflict*.   (verb, noun)

The tribes chose to *separate* into *separate* nations.   (verb, adjective)

The part of speech may differ, but the sound may stay the same.

That's a beautiful *stone* in your ring.   (noun)

I hate to *stone* cherries.   (verb)

I like this *stone* carving.   (adjective)

And sometimes only the meaning differs. The word *case* is a noun in all these sentences.

The lawyer refused to take the *case*.

The doctor thinks he has a bad *case* of measles.

Why not buy a whole *case*?

In your *case* I'll make an exception.

The sign is printed in lower-*case* letters—no capitals.

Of course, *case* can also be a verb. Doesn't the detective in the movies always *case* the layout of a building or area before moving in on the suspects?

We are familiar with all these simple words, and pay little attention as we use them in our daily speech and writing. Let's go on to some words that demand more attention, more analysis.

WORD STUDY: BUILDING BLOCKS

Some word elements or word parts are important building blocks in the English language. One example is *word* (Old English *wurd*).

This is used simply as *word*, and it also appears in *foreword, wordage, wordy, reword, guideword, watchword, wordless, password, wordplay*, and many others.

A very common word element is *dict-*, from the Latin *dicere*, "to say, to speak (words)."

We see this in *dictator*, meaning someone whose word is law.

An office manager may *dictate* a letter or use a *dictaphone*.

Diction usually means choice of words. And we know about *dictionaries*.

Add *bene*, meaning good, and you have *benediction*, a blessing.

Or add *vale*, meaning farewell, and you have a word you know: *valedictorian*—the best student in the class, who says the class farewell to the old school.

And there are other, less common, words containing the word element *dict-*.

Let's take another Latin word, *ego*, meaning the self, I, I myself.

We say "My *ego* was badly hurt by this incident." We mean our sense of self, our pride.

Or we can say, "He certainly has a big *ego*." (He thinks very well of himself.) "What an *egotist*! Such *egotism*!" (Or *egoist*, and *egoism*.)

Some of us may be a bit *egocentric*, centered around ourselves.

But if egotism goes too far, it becomes *egomania*! Then it's time to drop such an acquaintance or recommend a psychiatrist.

One Greek word, *archos*, meaning ruler, appears in English as both a prefix and a suffix.

The prefix, *arch-*, is seen in words like *archbishop, archenemy*, and *archfiend*.

The suffix, *-arch*, appears in *monarch, patriarch* (dominant old male), *matriarch* (dominant old female), and others.

As you become aware of the way words are put together, and as you increase your vocabulary in college, you'll become familiar with more of these building blocks.

WORD CHAINS

Making a word chain is a tricky task. In the chain below, we start with the word *monogamy*. The next word repeats the *-gamy* part and adds *bi-*, becoming *bigamy*. We go on in this way, repeating one part of each word to make the next one. (The pronunciations of the words are listed at the bottom of the page.) Follow the chain!

monogamy —————— (being married to one person)

(being married to two people) ═══ *bigamy*

bisexual ——————— (said of a plant or animal having
both male and female characteristics)

(preferring one's own sex) ═══ *homosexual*

heterosexual ════ (preferring the opposite sex)

(of different kinds) ═══ *heterogeneous*

homogeneous ════ (of the same kind)

(mass murder of one kind ═══ *genocide*
or race of people)

patricide ════ (murder of a father)

(dominant father figure) ═══ *patriarch*

monarch ════ (ruler who rules alone)

————— *monogamy*

Practice the pronunciations given below; then reread the word chain. Hear how the word parts are repeated. Note the meaning of each word part. A word chain can make you more aware of common word elements.

Now for the pronunciation of the words in the chain. Check each one with care before rereading the chain.

monogamy (mə nog′ə mē)   **homogeneous** (hō′mə jē′nē əs)
bigamy (big′ə mē)   **genocide** (jen′ə sīd′)
bisexual (bī sek′sho͞o əl)   **patricide** (pa′tri sīd′)
homosexual (hō′mə sek′sho͞o əl)   **patriarch** (pā′trē ärk′)
heterosexual (het′ər ə sek′sho͞o əl) **monarch** (mon′ərk)
heterogeneous (het′ər ə jē′nē əs)

PRONUNCIATION KEY: a*ct*, ā*ble*, dâ*re*, är*t;* e*bb*, ē*qual;* i*f*, ī*ce; h*o*t*, ō*ver*, ô*rder*, oil, ou*t;* up, û*rge*, ū*se;* bo͝ok, bo͞ot; ə = *a* in *alone;* sin̄g*;* s̠hoe*;* t̠hin, t̠hat*;* c̠hief*;* kept*;* go*;* just*;* zh = *s* in *measure*

PREFIXES WITH TWO OR MORE MEANINGS

Examine these dictionary entries. Each explains two or more meanings of a single prefix.

A. fore-
1. in front or near the front, as in *forehead*
2. beforehand, as in *foresee*

B. meta-
1. along with or among
2. after or behind
3. changed or changing

C. re-
1. once more, again, as in *reread*
2. backward, as in *reverse*

D. semi-
1. half, as in *semicircle*
2. partly, as in *semidivine*
3. twice, as in *semimonthly*

E. sub-
1. under, as in *subway*
2. of lesser importance, as in *subordinate*

EXERCISE 19   Selecting a Specific Meaning of a Prefix

Each sentence contains a word beginning with one of the prefixes defined above. In the right-hand column give the letter of the prefix and the number of the definition that fits the sentence. For the word *reverse*, for example, you would write C 2.

1. The Smiths' house was completely destroyed, but they plan to *rebuild* it in the very near future. _____

2. A caterpillar goes through quite a *metamorphosis* when it changes form and becomes a beautiful butterfly. _____

3. Though he was working in far-off Alaska, Jim managed to make *semiannual* visits to his hometown and his family. _____

4. Last night's news *forecast* that soon the United States will sign two new treaties was of considerable importance. _____

5. He is really just an unimportant *subofficial* in that big manufacturing company. _____

6. Mayor Jones was elected by a big majority, but now the voters are trying to *recall* her from office. _____

7. No, she doesn't have a fever; as a matter of fact, her temperature is *subnormal*. _____

WORD STUDY: NEGATIVES AND SUPERLATIVES

Many negative prefixes and suffixes appear in English words. Here are some of them: *non-, a-, im-, in-, un-, dis-, ir-, il-,* and *-less.*

We find these negative word parts in many of our very common words, and they can help us understand less common words that have these same parts.

EXERCISE 20   Locating Negative Prefixes and Suffixes

In the sentences below, locate the words that contain a negative prefix or suffix. Underline the negative word part in each case. *Notice the meaning.*

1. No, the chairperson was not pleased; in fact, he was highly displeased about the whole matter.

2. At the end of the sermon, the priest spoke so softly that the words were inaudible to many members of the audience.

3. Sorry, but I consider your remark in bad taste, and quite pointless besides.

4. He claimed to be extremely wealthy, but actually his wealth was nonexistent.

5. All we could see were a few words written on the rock in illegible handwriting, so we were quite disappointed.

6. He is neither moral nor immoral; he has no moral sense, so you might say he is amoral, like an animal.

7. In spite of the religious atmosphere of the occasion, they were talking and even laughing quite irreverently.

EXERCISE 21   Locating Positive Prefixes or Superlatives

Some prefixes, far from being negative, are strongly positive. For example: *super-, sur-, maxi-, extra-,* and *over-.*

In the following sentences, locate the words with these prefixes and underline the prefix. Notice the meaning, which is somewhat different for each prefix.

1. It's fine to be confident, but don't be overconfident.

2. My minimum is $100, and my maximum is $175.

3. Is this a natural event, or could it be a supernatural one?

4. It's really quite extraordinary the way Diana can tell what people are thinking— can it be extrasensory perception?

5. This picture is not just realistic; it's surrealistic, and very suggestive if you use your imagination.

EXERCISE 23   Review Page: Working with a Dictionary

Find the answers to these questions by consulting the dictionary entries on page 174. Work slowly and carefully.

1. Check the entry for *shan't*. What word or abbreviation tells you that this is a word commonly used in an informal way, as in conversation?   _____

2. Study the *shanty* entry.
   A. You are not told directly, but by reading the whole entry you will be able to guess the answer to this question: What were the first shanties probably made out of?   _____
   B. Where in your dictionary would you look to find synonyms for the word *shanty*?   _____

3. Note that there are two entries for *shark*. The first one is labeled "origin obscure"—the source is not known. What was the meaning of the German word from which *shark*² came?   _____

4. The *a* sound in the word *Shari* is like the *a* sound in one of these words. Which one?
         pair   car   dare   sham   hair   _____

5. Which meaning of *shark* would fit this sentence? Give the number of the definition.
         He's a real shark at mathematics.   _____

6. The word *sharp* has several similar meanings. Some of the noun meanings are especially close to each other. (The noun meanings start with 15). For instance, in the two sentences below the meanings are close together, but they are not quite the same. Give the number of the proper definition for each. (If you don't know what a *sharper* is, look up the word.)
   A. My good friend Jim is a real card sharp; I love to play with him.   _____
   B. That card sharp has cheated all of us; now he has disappeared.   _____

7. In what part of the world would you find a *sharpie*?   _____

8. What well-known organization includes among its members a number of *shavetails*? _____

9. Check the entries for the underlined words and give the correct definition number for each word as it is used in the sentence.

    A. *adj.*   Watch that <u>sharp</u> bend in the road, please, driver. _____

    B. *n.*   Wow! That was a close <u>shave</u>! _____

    C. *n.*   Tell the little <u>shaver</u> that his father is on the way. _____

A DICTIONARY ENTRY: the word *value*

val·ue (val′yo͞o), *n.*   **1.** a fair or proper equivalent in money or goods, for something sold or exchanged; fair price.   **2.** the worth of a thing in money or goods at a certain time; market price.   **3.** the equivalent of something in money: *She lost jewels to the value of* $10,000.   **4.** estimated or appraised price or worth; valuation.   **5.** purchasing power: *The value of the dollar changes.*   **6.** desirable or worthy of respect for its own sake; worth in this sense.   **7.** precise meaning, as of a word.   **8.** *Art.* the relative lightness or darkness of a color.   **9.** *Math.* the quality or amount for which a symbol stands.   **10.** *Phonetics.* the quality of a sound: *Each of the vowel sounds has several values in English.*   **11.** *Sociology.* the customs, institutions, and beliefs regarded in a particular, especially favorable, way by a people, ethnic group, etc. (used in the plural).   —*v.t.* **12.** to set a price for, estimate the value of, appraise.   **13.** to value one thing in relation to another; *to value health more than wealth.*   **14.** to think highly of, to esteem highly: *I value your friendship.*   —**Syn.** See **appreciate; worth**.

EXERCISE 24   Working with the Dictionary Entry for *value*

Value is a common word. But it has many meanings.

1. If we ask, "What's the value of a beautiful memory?,"
   the meaning we have in mind is explained by definition number _____

2. But if we say "What's the *value* of this old vase that I want to sell?,"

   the meaning we have in mind is explained by definition number _____

3. There are four fields in which the word *value*, used as a noun, has special meanings. Name these four fields.

   A. _____   C. _____

   B. _____   D. _____

4. Read this sentence.

       The *values* of this mountain tribe were very clear and strong.

   Values in this meaning occurs in the special field of _____

5. Study the use of the word *value*.

       We *value* the consideration that you've shown us.

   What part of speech is this? It's _____
   The dictionary entry for this use of the word shows the part of speech label

   _____

EXERCISE 25   Context Cues and Special Fields

Many common words are used in several different areas—law, science, sports—and
so have different meanings. The context of the sentences below tells you the area, and
it probably also tells you the general meaning of the word that fits the sentence.

I. The word <u>cast</u>, for example, can be used in different fields. There's
  A. theater   B. fishing   C. medicine   D. biology   E. general use
  Mark each of these sentences with the letter designating the field involved.

  1. _____   Roger had a *cast* on his arm for months.

  2. _____   The *cast* of the play gave a party for the director.

  3. _____   We *cast* our bait near the lily pads close to shore.

  4. _____   The snake *cast* its skin in this sunny spot.

  5. _____   Who will *cast* the first stone?

II. <u>Stock</u> can be either a noun or a verb, and in such varied fields as
  A. genealogy (human ancestry)   B. botany (the study of plants)
  C. cooking   D. guns   E. business   F. farming   G. finance and
  investments
  Mark each sentence with the letter for the field involved.

  1. _____   *Stock* is a plant of the mustard family.

  2. _____   Mary comes of good Irish *stock*.

  3. _____   This delicious soup has a special *stock* as its base.

  4. _____   The Adams store carries a big *stock* of men's shoes.

  5. _____   The *stock* of this expensive rifle is of polished teak.

  6. _____   A farmer must see that all his *stock* eat well and regularly.

  7. _____   He has all his money invested in common *stock*.

How does a word acquire so many meanings? Well, for one reason, it has
been in the language for a long time. In Middle English it was spelled *stocke*, and
way back in Old English times it was spelled *stocc*.

III. Now it's your turn. Read each sentence and decide what the topic is—what field the sentence is talking about. The word <u>line</u> is the key. Your answer might be just a simple, everyday word.

1. The Minnesota team has a good quarterback and a strong *line*. _____

2. The *line* in this store is mostly leather goods. _____

3. Drop me a *line* when you get to Paris. _____

4. Would you please hold the *line* for just a minute? _____

5. The FBI took the case because he had crossed the state *line*. _____

6. Only the Reading *line* runs to that city; the fare is a dollar. _____

7. Memorize the first fifty *lines* by Friday. _____

8. Since he lost that big fish, he uses a 30-pound test *line*. _____

9. He was stage-struck, terrified, and he forgot his *lines*. _____

10. A general is seldom found in the front *lines*. _____

The word *line* also has been in the language for a long time.

FLEXIBILITY
IN COLLEGE READING

FLEXIBILITY IN READING

The point of view and purpose of any piece of writing are important for you, as a reader, to understand. A flexible reading style will allow you to adapt to different purposes and viewpoints—to vary your own purpose, your speed, your attention. We read an advertisement more lightly than we read a textbook, for instance. We need to be *conscious* of our purpose in reading any given material.

A textbook is basically impersonal, in contrast to a letter from a friend, which is personal. Textbook writers are trying to give you organized information or the clear presentation of concepts (ideas), processes, procedures, facts. They try to be impartial, and usually they are.

A newspaper, on the other hand, generally reflects the point of view of the owner and management. A paper with a very conservative owner will reflect the owner's social and political attitudes in its editorials, in some of its features, and in much of its reporting. Most of the syndicated columns will not be very different. (A syndicated column is written by a well-known journalist. The right to reprint it regularly is purchased by the newspaper management, and management generally chooses the columns that are not too far from its point of view.) If there are a number of newspapers in a city, people choose the one that is closest to their own ideas and attitudes. They tend to read what they agree with.

The advertisements in newspapers and magazines have one purpose, and that is to persuade you of something—usually that you should buy a certain product. We sometimes read an advertisement uncritically and tend to believe its message without giving it much thought or analysis.

Magazines are designed to appeal to specific groups of readers. The *Pennsylvania Game News*, for example, clearly is for hunters interested in the latest developments in all aspects of hunting in Pennsylvania. This magazine is published by the Pennsylvania Game Commission. But most magazines are money-making enterprises, whether they aim to inform, entertain, or both. You should also be aware that some magazines are published by special-interest groups, religious or political or other, and represent the point of view of those groups. Such publications are bound to be slanted to some extent.

As you read a textbook, newspaper, or magazine, you must recognize the author's, editor's, or publisher's point of view and purpose. In the following pages we'll work with some short examples of common kinds of college reading material.

Your own point of view, your opinion of whatever is being discussed, is important —to you. But, when reading a textbook, you must keep your point of view quite separate from the point of view expressed in the material you're studying. In a classroom discussion, and occasionally on tests, you may be asked to express your own opinion. But generally, especially in beginning college courses, this does not happen in any very significant way. As you become acquainted with other points of view in your college reading, and as you acquire more knowledge, you may find yourself keeping the same opinions or you may find that they are changing a good deal.

In any case, learning to distinguish between various points of view—including your own—and developing a flexible reading style are among the most valuable achievements of a college education.

READING NEWSPAPERS

The editorials in a newspaper show its political and social point of view most clearly. The columns and features occasionally are done from the same point of view, though this may not be quite so clear-cut.

The special sections of a newspaper, called the features, might include a gardening column, a food section, movie and book reviews, and others. Such features make the paper attractive to readers with a variety of interests.

The special column reprinted below from the *Philadelphia Inquirer* has the general title "Investor Background." It is intended for readers of the paper who are interested in investments and in business generally.

The topic of this particular "Investor Background" column is shown in the subtitle: "C. of C. Begins Blitz Plan." C. of C. stands for Chamber of Commerce. Every sizable city has such a chamber, which represents local business interests. In this case, the C. of C. is the national Chamber of Commerce, representing American business nationwide.

When you read almost any part of a newspaper, it's a good idea to read it critically—that is, in a questioning way. Here's the column as it appeared in the *Inquirer*. Try to read it critically. (The word *blitz* is a military term suggesting a sudden large-scale attack.)

Investor Background

C. OF C. BEGINS BLITZ PLAN

[1]New and shifting pressures on the business community, including Americans' educational level and the growing number of working women, have provoked the U.S. Chamber of Commerce into a blitz information program. Beginning Tuesday in Greenville, S.C., and Detroit, Chamber speakers will visit 35 cities in 32 states in the next six weeks to arouse and educate business to some of these trends and the possible danger in them.

[2]The program, according to the national Chamber, is based partly on the fear that today's affluent, well educated and increasingly young population may be willing to sacrifice some freedom for security.

[3]A result of this—a result the Chamber feels is either imminent or already with us—is that the Federal Government will assume a greater role in business and the economy. This role, by its nature would be restrictive.

[4]Among the trends changing our society and exerting pressures on business, the Chamber lists these:

[5]"*Population*—it is changing. Young people will make up the greatest part of a big population growth, especially in the 1980s. More workers will be under 25. And the ratio of working women will rise sharply, from about one in three or four to one in two.

[6]"If business people wish to be heard effectively, they must be aware of and in touch with these new groups.

[7]"*Education*—in the depression thirties, only three in ten were high school graduates. Today the ratio is 7 in 10. . . . With better education, Americans are

From *The Philadelphia Inquirer*, February 15, 1967. Reprinted by permission.

developing rising expectations. They have stronger views about standards of performance for business. . . ."

[8]Few specific alternatives to these threats are offered. The Chamber places its reliance on the hope that people educated in free enterprise will defend it.

[9]Education, however, is the very thing the Chamber feels has swelled pressures.

[10]"But here comes another development—a push for Federal laws that are designed to protect the consumer. This development, we need to understand, grows in part out of two of the underlying trends:

[11]"The tremendous technological gains of the past 25 years or so; and the higher level of education is very much in the picture, too."

[12]These and other factors, the Chamber feels, mean the consumer is likely to be sympathetic toward proposals calling for Government standards and protection. And such intervention, if not delicately approached, could mean danger.

[13]The Chamber is also rating Senators and Representatives on whether they have voted in agreement or against the business community viewpoint, as measured by their own members.

[14]"This voting tabulation should be regarded as a report, not as an evaluation," the Chamber's literature notes. Since a judgment is made, however, it is an evaluation. It is, in fact, referred to elsewhere as a rating sheet.

[15]The Chamber says it hopes to arouse and inform business people about the key issues.

[16]"Concern about the state of affairs is meaningless without enlightened action," it concludes.

EXERCISE 1   Analyzing a Newspaper Column

This column, "C. of C. Begins Blitz Plan," reports almost entirely the point of view of the Chamber of Commerce, which represents business. The column focuses mostly on the Chamber's worry about three "new groups" in American Society: (1) the increasing number of young people, (2) the greater number of educated people, especially young people, and (3) working women in larger numbers.

1. The Chamber seems to be in a state of alarm over the existence of these three groups in American society. The Chamber expresses "fear" because of "pressures," "danger," and "threats" from these new groups. The Chamber's attitude toward these groups may be due to
   A. genuine concern for the welfare of these people
   B. concern for the welfare of businesses that employ these people
   C. concern that these workers may make greater demands on business

   Probably A, B, or C? _____

2. In paragraph 12 we read about "Government standards and protection." Protection for whom? For
   A. the Chamber of Commerce
   B. the business community in the United States
   C. American consumers   Which? _____

3. The Chamber has prepared for the business people who are its members a rating sheet showing which Senators and Representatives have voted for the business point of view and which have voted against it. On the basis of the information in the rating sheet, what action might the Chamber members logically take? <u>Two</u> of these suggestions make the best sense.
   A. They might get personally acquainted with their Senators.
   B. They might try to influence those who have voted against business.
   C. They might vote against those who have voted against business.
   D. They might try to influence the national government as a whole.
   E. They might report back to the national Chamber.

   Which two? _____

4. The attitude of the passage, as we've seen, is mostly that of the Chamber of Commerce. But the attitude of the writer of the column is shown once, in
   A. paragraph 1, sentence 2   C. paragraph 10, sentence 1
   B. paragraph 12, sentence 1   D. paragraph 14, sentences 2 and 3

5. On the basis of what is said in the passage about education, how would the Chamber be likely to feel about a big-city community college with low tuition and open admissions? The Chamber of Commerce would probably feel
   A. hopeful   B. anxious   C. admiring   D. paternalistic (like a father)

   Which seems likely? _____

READING ADVERTISEMENTS

Advertisements are an important source of financial support for newspapers and magazines. They're important also to the companies that advertise.

Here's a newspaper advertisement that was used to introduce a new product. Study the advertisement. Notice the way it tries to persuade you to buy this product.

It's the American way to enjoy Fish 'n Chips.

Mrs. Paul's has taken a traditional
English favorite and turned it into a new American sensation.
Tender, tasty fish fillets under a
delicately seasoned breading. Plus chips (potatoes)
that are plump and round and crispy.

Just heat and serve, topped off with Mrs. Paul's
own Create a Sauce Mix that's included right in the package.
They're great for dinner. For lunch. For snacks.

Quality from *Mrs. Paul's* Kitchens

STORE COUPON

10¢ OFF

**This coupon good for 10¢ off
when you buy a package
of *Mrs. Paul's* Fish 'n Chips.**

NOTICE TO GROCER: For each coupon you accept as our authorized agent, we will pay you face value, plus 3¢ for handling, provided you and your customer have complied with the terms of this offer. This coupon is good only when redeemed by you from a consumer at time of purchasing specified products. This coupon is non-assignable. Invoices proving purchase of sufficient stock to cover coupons presented for redemption must be shown upon request. (Failure to comply may void all coupons submitted for redemption.) The consumer must pay any sales tax. This offer limited to one coupon per specified product and size. Void if prohibited by law, taxed or restricted. Cash value 1/20 of 1¢. Send to Mrs. Paul's Kitchens, P. O. Box 1725, Clinton, Iowa 52734. Expires March 31, 1975.

EXERCISE 2 Examining a Newspaper Advertisement

The main aim of the advertisement for Fish'n Chips clearly is to persuade you to try this new product of Mrs. Paul's.

The writer of the ad tries in a number of ways to persuade you to buy some Fish'n Chips. For example, at the very beginning of the ad we are told that Mrs. Paul's is proud of the new product. The fact that they are proud of it is supposed to make us feel that the product must be good.

See how many other ways of persuading us you can find. There are quite a few.

1. _____

2. _____

3. _____

4. _____

5. _____

6. _____

7. _____

8. _____

9. _____

10. _____

Which of these ways of persuasion do *you* find most attractive? Which of the points you've listed might convince you that you should try Fish'n Chips?

Number _____ and also numbers _____

Do you think it is easy to write such an advertisement? Probably not. A lot of thought goes into writing an ad. This product was a new one, and whether or not it sold may have depended quite a bit on the advertisement.

As readers and as consumers, all of us must study advertisements carefully.

READING MAGAZINES

Millions of Americans read magazines. For those interested in sports, there are *Field and Stream*, *Rod and Gun*, and a dozen others. For the house or apartment owner, there's *American Home* and others like it. For the business executive, the stamp collector, the physician, there's a magazine, or maybe ten or more. Readers select the ones that suit their interests and points of view.

Look at copies of some of the magazines listed below, in your college library or at a newsstand. Then select one that's of special interest to you. You'll be answering an essay-type question on the magazine you choose, so take your time in making your selection.

What are the *facts* about the magazine you've chosen? As you examine a copy, take very precise factual notes. This is the first step toward writing about your magazine, since you'll be using the notes to answer the essay question.

Organize your notes by topic. Here are some topics to consider.

- √ Is your magazine published by some special group, such as the Peace Corps? Or is it, like most magazines, published for profit?
- √ What kind of advertisements does it have? Note some specific ads. Do the ads in general suggest that the readers are rich, middle-class, or poor?
- √ Is the magazine itself expensive or inexpensive?
- √ Does it use cartoons, photographs, illustrations, charts? Find some that seem to be typical examples of those used in your particular magazine.
- √ What subjects does it cover? Politics? Science? Homemaking? Note the titles of two or three typical articles.
- √ Does it have any regular features, such as editorials, letters from readers, book reviews, that appear in every issue? Note two or three of these.
- √ Are there any really unusual angles about your particular magazine? For example, a few magazines carry no ads at all, and some are mostly pictures.

As you examine your magazine, think about the reader who subscribes to it or buys it regularly. Who is this person? The articles will tell you. So will the advertisements. Ads for Cadillacs and European resorts will have one audience. Ads for canned soup and paper towels have a different audience. Each magazine has its own point of view and its own readers.

Choose one of these magazines—but please pick one you're *not* familiar with.

Atlas	*Ms.*
Black Careers	*Philadelphia*
Business Week	*Soviet Life*
Harper's Bazaar	*Sports Illustrated*
Holiday	*Vista*

Be sure you collect a solid body of notes. If you are examining your magazine in the library, check to see that your notes are complete before you leave. Remember, you'll use the notes as you write about the magazine.

Write your notes in the spaces provided on page 191. But *first* study page 190. The sample notes and essay answer there will show you the kind of notes you need and how you will use them in writing about your magazine.

DISCOVERING THE AUDIENCE OF A MAGAZINE

Magazines are particularly important to college students as sources of information for written reports. Term papers must often deal with topics of *current* interest—and magazines are your best sources.

But in using a magazine for a college report, you must recognize its point of view. For example, suppose you quote from *Commonweal*, a Roman Catholic lay publication, on the subject of birth control. You must then have other sources in order to give a balanced view. If you want to be objective, you can't cite just one side of a question.

So recognizing the audience and point of view of a magazine is important to college students. That's what we're practicing here.

Before taking notes on your magazine, read over the sample notes and the short paragraph that follow.

Notes on *Woman Today*

<u>publisher</u>:   Anderson Enterprises, Inc.

<u>ads</u>:   Vogue patterns, Super Sheen, Femina, Max Makeup, Wilton Fabrics

<u>articles</u>:   "The Problem of Food Additives," "Educational Testing and Black Children," "Computers Today," "Those Beautiful African Women"

<u>illustrations</u>:   photographs of three African women in evening gowns; photo of Sarah Vaughan; photos and sketches of the newest styles

<u>features</u>:   Write On (letters from readers), Style Trends, Consumer Reports, Sounds, The Political Front, *Woman Today*'s Black Man of the Month

QUESTION: What type of American reads the magazine you have studied?

ANSWER: *Woman Today* is published for the style-conscious black woman. Her interest in style is shown by such articles as "Those Beautiful African Women" and by the many advertisements for products like Super Sheen, Femina hair products, Max Makeup, and Wilton Fabrics. One special feature, Style Trends, with its photographs and sketches of the latest fashions, shows her interest in stylish clothes. There are also the full-page photographs of three beautiful African women wearing full-length evening gowns. The black woman who reads this magazine obviously has some money to spend on clothes and similar products, since many of the products advertised are rather expensive—Vogue patterns, for example, are more expensive than most other patterns. Her interest in black personalities is shown by the article on Sarah Vaughan, accompanied by a large photograph, and by the feature called *Woman Today*'s Black Man of the Month. It's clear that this black woman has broader interests too. Look at the titles of these articles: "Educational Testing and Black Children," "The Problem of Food Additives," and "Computers Today." Several features also show varied interests: Consumer Reports, Sounds, and the Political Front. The black woman who reads this magazine is someone I'd like to meet.

Note that the examples given in the answer are *specific*: specific products, like Super Sheen, and specific articles, like "Computers Today."

TAKING NOTES ON A MAGAZINE

Write your notes on the magazine you have chosen in the spaces below.

The publisher's name might be printed in small type and hard to find, but this information is required by law to be in every issue of a magazine. Look on the first page after the cover or on one of the following pages.

In your handwritten notes or on the typewriter, the titles of magazines should be underlined. (On a printed page the titles would be in *italics*.) In your notes and in your paragraph, remember to underline the magazine title, no matter how many times you write it. But the titles of articles in the magazine should have quotation marks around them.

Publisher: _____

Advertisements that are typical: _____

_____

_____

Cost of the magazine per issue: _____

Titles of typical articles: _____

_____

_____

_____

_____

Illustrations, cartoons, drawings, etc.: _____

_____

_____

_____

_____

Features, special sections: _____

_____

_____

_____

_____

HOW TO ANALYZE A MAGAZINE

Now you are ready to write an essay-type answer to a question on your magazine. Use your notes as you write.

An educational authority has given this advice to students:

In writing essay-type tests, students should be very careful to answer each question precisely in the very first sentence: illustrations, examples, and further discussion should be included only after the question has been answered directly.

This advice applies to the essay-type answer you'll write now.

Imagine this situation:
In a course in contemporary American society, you have been analyzing the various groups and interests within our society today. You have personally studied one current American magazine that reflects the interests of one kind of American.

Your examination question is this:

What special type of person in American society today is likely to read the magazine you have studied? What is there about the magazine—the articles or advertisements or whatever—that tells you that the magazine appeals to this kind of American?

Answer this question in ONE well-organized paragraph.

Remember the importance of using specific examples and details to support your general statements.

Look back at the paragraph on *Woman Today* if you like. This may help you to realize how important specific examples are in an essay answer like this one.

Write your paragraph on page 193, using the notes you wrote on page 191.

Name_____ Date_____

EXERCISE 3   Analyzing the Audience of a Magazine

_____

_____

_____

_____

_____

_____

_____

_____

_____

_____

_____

_____

_____

_____

_____

_____

_____

_____

_____

_____

_____

Always—always—check your answer before handing in your paper.

READING AN AUTOBIOGRAPHY

Frequently, as a college student, you will be required to study books, poems, or other readings from the past—sometimes the distant past. Always you must attempt to keep in mind when and where the passage was written, whether in Greece in the fifth century before Christ or in England ten years ago.

To most Americans, our past—the American past—is of the greatest interest. One dark period in our history as a nation was the long era of slavery. Let's take a look into the past and see slavery in action.

Frederick Douglass, the American abolitionist and orator, was born a slave. In 1855, after a heroic and distinguished career as a campaigner for the Massachusetts Anti-Slavery Society, he wrote *My Bondage and My Freedom*.

Here we have a glimpse into the American past—as seen through the eyes of a young slave boy. Use your imagination and put yourself in his place as you read. Remember, he was six or seven years old at the beginning of this story, and he was a slave.

Follow along as young Frederick gradually realizes his true situation as a slave and sees what slavery itself has done to his owner and also to himself.

MY BONDAGE AND MY FREEDOM

Established in my new home in Baltimore, I was not very long in perceiving that in picturing to myself what was to be my life there, my imagination had painted only the bright side; and that the reality had its dark shades as well as its light ones . . . .

Mrs. Sophia was naturally of an excellent disposition—kind, gentle, and cheerful. The contempt for the rights and feelings of others, and the bad humor which generally characterized slaveholding ladies, were all quite absent from her manner and bearing toward me.

She had never been a slaveholder—a thing then quite unusual in the South—but had depended almost entirely upon her own industry for a living. To this fact the dear lady no doubt owed the excellent preservation of her natural goodness of heart, for slavery could change a saint into a sinner, and an angel into a demon. . . . So far from deeming it impudent in a slave to look her straight in the face, she seemed ever to say, "Look up, child; don't be afraid." . . . Mr. Hugh was altogether a different character. He cared very little about religion, knew more of the world, and was more a part of the world than his wife. He doubtless set out to be, as the world goes, a respectable man and to get on by becoming a successful ship-builder, in that city of ship-building. This was his ambition, and it fully occupied him. Though I must in truth characterize Master Hugh as a sour man of forbidding appearance, it is due to him to acknowledge that he was never cruel to me, according to the notion then of cruelty, in Maryland. During the first year or two, he left me almost exclusively to the management of his wife. She was my law-giver. . . . My employment was to run errands, and to take care of her son Tommy; to prevent his getting in the way of carriages, and to keep him out of harm's way generally.

So for a time everything went well. . . . The frequent hearing of my mistress reading the Bible aloud, for she often read aloud when her husband was absent, awakened my curiosity about this *mystery* of reading, and roused in me the desire to learn. With an unconsciousness and inexperience equal to my own, she readily consented to teach me; and in an incredibly short time, by her kind assistance, I had mastered the alphabet and could spell words of three or four letters. My mistress seemed almost as proud of my progress as if I had been her own child, and supposing that her husband would be as well pleased, she made no secret of what she was doing for me. Indeed, she told him of the aptness of her pupil and of her intention to continue, as she felt it her duty to do so, in teaching me, at least, to read the Bible. And here arose the first dark cloud over my Baltimore prosepcts, the first of chilling blasts and drenching storms.

Master Hugh was astounded beyond measure and, probably for the first time, proceeded to unfold to his wife the true philosophy of the slave system, and the peculiar rules necessary to be observed in the case of human property. Of course he forbade her to give me any further instruction, telling her in the first place that to do so was unlawful, as it was also unsafe; "for," said he, "learning will spoil the best nigger in the world. If he learns to read the Bible it will forever unfit him to be a slave. He should know nothing but the will of his master, and learn to obey it. As to himself, learning will do him no good, but a great deal of harm, making him disconsolate and unhappy. If you teach him how to read, he'll want to know how to write, and this accomplished, he'll be running away with himself." Such was the content of Master Hugh's remarks; and it must be confessed that he very clearly comprehended the requirements of the relation of master and slave. This was the first decidedly anti-slavery lecture to which it had been my lot to listen. Mrs. Auld evidently felt the force of what he said, and like an obedient wife, began to shape her actions in the direction indicated by him. The effect of his words *on me* was neither small nor temporary. His iron sentences, cold and harsh, sunk like heavy weights deep into my heart, and stirred up within me a rebellion not soon to be satisfied.

This was new and special knowledge, dispelling a painful mystery against which my youthful mind had struggled, and struggled in vain—the white man's power to maintain the enslavement of the black man. "Very well," thought I. "Knowledge unfits a child to be a slave." I instinctively agreed to the proposition that this was true, and from that moment I understood the direct pathway from slavery to freedom. It was just what I needed, and it came to me at a time and from a source whence I least expected it. Of course, I was greatly saddened at the thought of losing the assistance of my kind mistress, but the information I had just acquired to some extent made up for this loss. Wise as Mr. Auld was, he underrated my comprehension of what he had said, and had little idea of the use to which I was capable of putting the lesson he was giving to his wife. . . .

I lived in the family of Mr. Auld seven years. The most interesting feature of my history here was my learning, under somewhat marked disadvantages, to read and write. I was compelled to resort to concealments by no means pleasing to my nature, and which were really humiliating to my sense of candor and uprightness. My mistress, checked in her kind designs toward me, not only ceased instructing me herself, but set her face against my learning to read by any means. It is due to her to say, however, that she did not adopt this course fully at first. She was, as I have said, naturally a kind and tender-hearted woman, and in the humanity of her heart and the simplicity of her mind, she set out, when I first went to live with her, to treat me as she supposed one human being ought to treat another. . . .

But slavery soon proved its ability to take from her these excellent qualities, and from her home its early happiness. Conscience cannot stand much violence. Once thoroughly injured, who is he who can repair the damage? If conscience be broken toward the slave on Sunday, it will be toward the master on Monday. It cannot long endure such shocks. It must stand unharmed, or not at all.

As my condition in the family became bad, that of the family became no better. In ceasing to instruct me, my mistress had to seek to justify herself *to* herself, and once taking sides in such a debate, she had to hold her position. She finally became even more violent in her opposition to my learning to read than Mr. Auld himself. Nothing now appeared to make her more angry than seeing me, seated in some nook or corner, quietly reading a book or newspaper. She would rush at me with the utmost fury, and snatch the book or paper from my hand, with something of the anger which a traitor might feel on being discovered in a plot by some dangerous spy. Once she was convinced in her mind that education and slavery were incompatible with each other, I was most closely watched in all my movements. If I remained in a separate room from the family for any length of time, I was sure to be suspected of having a book, and was called to give an account of myself. But this was too late; the first and never-to-be-retraced step had been taken. . . .

Filled with the determination to learn to read at any cost, I hit upon many expedients to accomplish that much desired end. . . . When I was about thirteen years old, and had succeeded in learning to read, every increase of knowledge, especially anything about the free states, was an additional weight to the almost unbearable burden of my thought—"*I am a slave for life.*" To my bondage I could see no end. It was a terrible reality, and I shall never be able to tell how sadly that thought hurt my young spirit. Fortunately, I had, by blacking boots for some gentlemen, earned a little money with which I purchased what was then a very popular school book, *The Columbian Orator*, for which I paid fifty cents. . . .

Here was indeed a noble acquisition. If I had ever wavered under the idea that the Almighty, in some way, had ordained slavery and willed my enslavement for His own glory, I wavered no longer. I had penetrated to the secret of all slavery and of all oppression, and had learned their true foundation to be in the pride, the power, and the greed of man. With a book in my hand so full of the principles of liberty, and wih a knowledge of my own human nature and the facts of my past and present experience, I was ready for an argument with the religious advocates of slavery, whether white or black; for blindness in this matter was not confined to the white people. I have met, in the South, many good, religious colored people who were under the delusion that God required them to submit to slavery and to wear their chains with meekness and humility. I could entertain no such nonsense as this, and I quite lost my patience when I found a colored man weak enough to believe such stuff. . . .

I have no doubt that my state of mind had something to do with the change of treatment that my mistress adopted toward me. I can easily believe that my downcast and disconsolate look was very offensive to her. Poor lady! She did not understand my trouble, and I could not tell her. Nature made us friends, but slavery made us enemies. She aimed to keep me ignorant, and I resolved to *know*, although knowledge only increased my misery.

My feelings were not the result of any marked cruelty in the treatment I received; they sprang from the consideration of my being a slave at all. It was *slavery* I hated. I saw through the attempt to keep me in ignorance. I saw that slaveholders would have gladly made me believe that, in making a slave of me, and in making slaves of others, they were merely acting under the authority of God, but I felt of them that they were robbers and deceivers. The feeding and clothing of me well could not atone for taking my liberty from me. The smiles of my mistress could not remove the deep sorrow that dwelt in my young bosom. Indeed, these came, in time, to deepen my sorrow. She had changed, and the reader will see that I, too, had changed. We were both victims of the same overshadowing evil, she as mistress, I as slave. I will not censure her too harshly.

EXERCISE 4   Looking Back at "My Bondage and My Freedom"

1. Reading this account of a child slave, we see changes in the boy himself.

    He had been _____

    He became _____
    When did he become determined to educate himself, to "know"?

    _____

2. We also see changes in Mrs. Auld.

    She had been _____

    She became _____

    She was changed by _____

3. Looking back at his days as a young slave boy, Frederick Douglass is generous in
    his understanding of the change in Mrs. Auld's treatment of him. He does not
    blame Mrs. Auld herself for what happened. Who or what, in his opinion, is to
    blame?

    _____

4. Why, according to Douglass, did some blacks accept slavery as their lot in life?

    _____

5. Some slaves were poorly clothed, poorly fed, and cruelly treated. How was the boy

    Frederick clothed and fed? _____ Treated?_____

6. What did young Frederick suddenly understand as the result of hearing Mr.
    Auld's remarks to his wife forbidding her to teach the boy to read?

    _____

    _____

7. Mr. Auld was obviously in favor of slavery. Yet Douglass says of Auld's remarks
    to his wife: "This was the first decidedly anti-slavery lecture to which it had been
    my lot to listen." Can you guess why Douglass considered this an *anti*-slavery

    lecture? _____

    _____

    _____

READING AN ARTICLE

When Clifton Fadiman wrote "The Great Debate on Education," he was reacting to a historical event that had recently been reported in the newspapers.

SOVIETS LAUNCH SATELLITE

October 4, 1957—Early reports indicate that the Soviet Union has launched an unmanned space satellite called Sputnik. It is now in orbit and is being monitored from several stations in the United States.

American space experts on both coasts have indicated they knew of Soviet advances in the space field but were unprepared for this early launching. There is no indication that the American space establishment will be able to launch a satellite of its own in the immediate future.

When the American space establishment eventually did attempt to launch a satellite, it was a failure. "Sputternik" was its nickname. "We've fallen behind the Russians!" Americans whispered—or shouted. A national demand for more and better technical education, for more engineers, followed immediately. Meanwhile, with Sputnik II, the Soviets took a further step—a dog was sent into space.

During the period of American reaction, Fadiman wrote the article you are about to read. It reflects his view of the situation at the time it was written, in 1957, and was published in *Holiday*, a travel magazine, in August 1958. As you read the article, bear in mind these questions:

Is this article, written in 1957, still meaningful today?

Do you think that the later, successful American space program has changed American attitudes toward education?

What is Fadiman's method here? Is it, for example, basically factual?

As you read, notice the three *footnotes*, which have been added to explain some of Fadiman's references. Many of the articles and books you study in college will have footnotes. Usually a footnote explains a reference or gives the source of a fact or quotation; it may also present additional information.

THE GREAT DEBATE ON EDUCATION

[1]At the Madison High School in Rochester, New York, twelve-year-old boys are forced to take a course in coeducational "homemaking," including diapering. In another, in California, scholastic credit is given to students for working as carry-out boys in supermarkets. There is another California school in which teenage lads attend a class called "Bachelor Living." A Maryland high school proudly announces that it offers the only course in dry cleaning in the county system. A high school in Schenectady, New York, boasts five gymnasiums, plus other educational paraphernalia, including a retail store and a classroom devoted to something called, simply, "Living"; its faculty socializes with the children in a "faculty-student lounge"; and the nonacademic part of the school (comprising 80 per cent of the available space) is air-conditioned, whereas the academic classes are not, presumably on the theory that any child so vicious as actually to prefer education to cosmetology should be penalized for this aberration. In San Francisco's City College a course labeled "Humanities" guarantees that "emphasis is also given to art in everyday life—for example, the appropriate selection of neckties and socks by the men of the class, and of dresses and costume jewelry by the women." Somebody named Ken Miller, according to the Champaign-Urbana *Courier*, expects shortly to receive his master's degree for a thesis on football punting. . . .

[2]Horrified? Or, perhaps, merely moved to derisive laughter? If so, you—and that includes the writer—are horrified at yourself, or laughing at yourself. For these enormities are precisely what we ordered. Each time, during the last twenty-five years, that we voted for a school bond issue to provide our children with a swimming pool instead of an acquaintance with the multiplication table; each time that we taxed ourselves to guarantee hot lunches for the kiddies and a continuance of starvation salaries for the teachers; each time that we failed to cry bloody murder when a report-card system was abolished, or compulsory promotion introduced: at each of these moments we were making dead sure that our children would turn out to be—what they are. We knew what we wanted: the garroting* of the mind. And we got it.

[3]The Great Debate on education, now raging all over the land, may turn out to be as important as the Lincoln-Douglas debates, or even those that preceded the adoption of the Constitution. No matter how it is decided, it is apparent that our school system is going to be improved. It is crystal-clear that from now on almost as much attention will be paid to the encouragement of a genius as we devote at present to the wet-nursing of the retarded. But the issue is not the improvement of the school system. The issue is the improvement of our minds. And our minds cannot improve unless we first rid ourselves of a few comforting delusions.

[4]I have touched on the first. It is the delusion that at the bottom of the trouble is a Villain; and that if we can only find this Villain and chastise him, all will be rosy. *Life*† has of late been doing a superb job of pointing out the flaws in our

---

* Garroting was a Spanish method of execution by means of an iron collar gradually tightened, causing strangulation.
† *Life*, a popular news and picture magazine, now discontinued.

school system. But, the livelier journalism of our time having become a branch of the dramatic art, *Life* had to uncover something and someone for us to hiss: a desperate doctrine called Progressive Education and a Desperate Desmond called John Dewey.‡

⁵Now, if you are looking for an indignation vent, these will do; but if you are looking for something duller, namely the truth, they will not. . . . The guilt must be assigned to a widely held theory of human life, a theory championed, in varying degrees of intensity, by all of us. There is a villain; seek him in your mirror.

⁶The theory of human life which has become the unconscious philosophy of most Americans is simply a perversion of the Constitutional phrase guaranteeing our right to pursue happiness. By happiness the Founding Fathers, who were well educated, meant more or less what Aristotle did. Happiness for them was a state of mind ensuing when one was sufficiently wise to make the right moral choices. It was associated with wisdom and morality.

⁷In our time it has become equivalent, to use a peculiarly American phrase, to "having a good time." If you doubt this, ask the average teen-ager (and we have seen to it, of course, that as many of them as possible will *be* average) what he wants out of life. It will boil down to two things: "a good time" and "security." And the average grownup will agree. . . .

⁸In education this idolization of the Good Time is translated into the child-centered school; into an elective system gone insane, to the point where a high-school graduate will choose a college because it offers sailing; into the religious enshrinement of athletics; and so forth. Once we accept, as we obviously do, the Good Time Theory of happiness it is inevitable that our children, instead of being taught how to read, write, speak and reason, will be taught how to train dogs, use the telephone, play in the school band, wield drum-majorette batons and select socks. . . .

⁹But some of us, reactionary old fogies, may feel that happiness—real happiness, the kind of happiness the Founding Fathers were talking about—is not a packageable commodity to be given away to the kiddies at those gigantic supermarkets masquerading as educational institutions.

¹⁰The second delusion that must be dissipated before the Great Debate can produce its finest fruits is the curious notion that the debate has just started. Forty-three years ago John Erskine published a book called *The Moral Obligation to be Intelligent*. We did not recognize the obligation. Twenty-five years ago a group of educators, among them Robert M. Hutchins, Mortimer Adler and Mark Van Doren, were urging a return to the liberal tradition in education and warning us that the enshrinement of athletics and vocational courses could lead only to the intellectual impoverishment of the nation. They were ignored or howled down. And, three years before the arrival of Sputnik, Arthur Bestor had surveyed our educational system, told us what was wrong, and been discounted as an extremist. The truth has been before us for at least a generation; we closed our eyes to it.

¹¹What opened them? Insight? Remorse? Reflection? Not any of these. Our eyes were opened by a flying box containing a dying dog. We are going to

‡ Progressive education concentrated less on rote learning and more on the child and his interests. John Dewey was an educational philosopher who was in part responsible for this development. "Desperate Desmond" was a comic-strip villain who twirled his moustache and laughed evilly as he tied the heroine to the railroad tracks.

reform American education not because we are eager to produce fine American citizens but because we are scared stiff. Whatever changes we make in our schooling will consequently be changes spurred on by a respect for the Russians rather than a respect for the intelligence. Let us see the Great Debate in perspective and admit that what the reformers have been urging for the last fifty years is only loosely connected with what is today being urged by the newer reformers.

[12]This brings us to the third delusion. That is the notion that our basic weakness is in something vaguely called "the sciences"; if we can only improve our mathematics and physics courses and attract to them a greater proportion of able students, all may yet be well. This delusion is the most dangerous because it seems to be connected with concrete things, such as space satellites, intercontinental ballistic missiles, and improved bombs, of all degrees of sanitariness. And as for at least twenty-five years our schools have been pooh-poohing abstract thought and cheering for concrete objects, it is probable that the physics-and-arithmetic reforms will go through, and that nothing else will.

[13]Now let us suppose that we have divested ourselves of these three delusions. We are now at least in a position to do some deciding. We may decide, as many educators in the secret, sad depths of their hearts have already decided, that the cultural jig is up; that the pressures of the modern world, the crushing competition of the entertainment trade and the athletics business, our present tendency to spawn on the level of the lower animals—that all these make impossible a return to traditional liberal education, guided by first-rate teachers. If that is our decision—and there is much evidence to sustain it—we should at once organize our degeneracy with the efficiency peculiar to us as a people. More swimming pools, more bowling alleys, more courses in dog training, more schools devoted to making children happy, more colleges functioning as a combination of health resort, country club and mating seminary; with perhaps special inducements held out to future technologists who may be useful for the defense of the country.

[14]But suppose we should decide the other way. Suppose we conclude that the Founding Fathers had a good idea after all, that a republic of free men (which means men with liberated minds) is worth striving for, even in the face of apparently insuperable obstacles. What do we do then?

[15]The answer is so simple as to seem impossible. We change our minds. . . . The change involves so radical an alteration of our folkways and mindways that the chances are a thousand to one against its succeeding. But unless we try it, on a national scale, we may as well abandon our schools to the vocationalists, the life-adjusters, the Happiness Boys. . . .

[16]Changing our minds basically involves agreeing with Aristotle, who tells us that all men by nature desire to know. *All* men—not some. By *nature*—not passive acceptance of instruction. If we do not accept this—then back to the gymnasiums and the classes in baton twirling.

[17]Another of Aristotle's dicta is "Education is accompanied by pain." This, too, we must accept. T. S. Eliot tells us "No one can become really educated without having pursued some study in which he took no interest—for it is a part of education to learn to interest ourselves in subjects for which we have no aptitude." If this be true, it makes hay of our elective system in which the student selects courses as if he were choosing penny candy in a candy store.

[18]The prestige symbols must be changed. Somehow or other, the child will

have to be taught the stark, chilly truth—that the intellectual is and always has been the most valuable human being in the world, the one on whom we all live, the one whose ideas and discoveries and inventions afford us the opportunity for a livelihood and show us how interesting life can be. It is only when he deeply feels the truth of this that his natural desire to know will express itself freely, and he will learn what it is now difficult to teach him—how to read, write, calculate, speak, listen, and think.

EXERCISE 5   Examining "The Great Debate on Education"

Bear in mind that this article was published during the period of American reaction
to the Russian launching of Sputnik, the satellite that showed Russian superiority
in space science at that time. Americans were, as Fadiman says in the article,
"scared stiff," and began to demand educational reform.

1. The article opens with a list of "enormities," or outrages—educational practices
   that Fadiman considers to be extremely bad, bad as education and bad for our
   nation. In using examples such as courses in bachelor living and cosmetology
   (the science of using cosmetics), Fadiman is taking something for granted:
   A. that educational theory of the time supports his view of these courses and his
      view of American life
   B. that educators will rise up and join him in taking action to see that these
      courses are eliminated
   C. that his readers will join him in his attitude of outrage at the existence of such
      courses in American schools
                                                  Which, A, B, or C? _____

The *language* of the article is interesting. Choice of words is important. For example,
Fadiman calls the ideas that he opposes "delusions," false beliefs.

2. "Supermarkets" in paragraph 9 is an attack on one aspect of American
   education that he has criticized at several points in the article. He compares a
   school to a supermarket, where you select the products you want as you go along.
   What he is attacking here is
   A. "the religious enshrinement of athletics"
   B. "idolization of the Good Time"
   C. "an elective system gone insane"   A, B, or C? _____

3. "A flying box containing a dying dog" is the phrase he uses in paragraph 11 to
   describe the Russian achievement in launching Sputnik II. This odd description
   of a scientific achievement is intended to give us the idea that
   A. the achievement is a purely technical one and so not of the very first
      importance in terms of a national culture
   B. sending a dog off into space in a container is an amazing scientific achievement
      of the very first order
   C. this experiment on the part of the Russians was intended only as a joke

                                                  A, B, or C? _____

4. Irony is saying the opposite of what you mean. To use a word ironically is to use it to mean the opposite of what it usually means. If we say "You're a *big* help!" we may mean that the person is not being helpful at all. Choose the word below that Fadiman uses to mean the opposite of what it usually means.
   A. vicious (paragraph 1, line 12)
   B. horrified (paragraph 2, line 1)
   C. delusion (paragraph 4, line 1) _____

Sometimes the *exact meaning* of a word or phrase is important. Try to figure out the exact meaning of the words or phrases given in the next three questions.

5. "We" in paragraph 2, lines 3 and 4, means
   A. the writer and any reader
   B. parents in the United States and children in the schools
   C. the American people who have voted as he says they have _____

6. "The last twenty-five years," in this particular essay, means
   A. 1933 to 1958
   B. the twenty-five years before today's date
   C. the twenty-five years before Erskine, Hutchins, Adler, and Mark Van Doren

   _____

7. "Too" in paragraph 17, line 2, means
   A. in addition to the wise saying of Aristotle
   B. in addition to the idea that all men desire to know
   C. in addition to the idea that education is accompanied by pain _____

The *references* of an article are part of its overall meaning and impact. Writers may refer to the Bible or the wise sayings of Buddha, to Napoleon, or to Lincoln. Usually there's a reason for each reference.

8. Fadiman refers to Aristotle, the famous Greek philosopher, in paragraphs 6, 16, and 17. He does this because
   A. he admires Aristotle's literary style
   B. he just wants to impress us with a famous name
   C. Aristotle has something to say that he considers important _____

9. In paragraph 3, "the Lincoln-Douglas debates, or . . . those that preceded the adoption of the Constitution" is a comparison used by Fadiman in order to
   A. show the importance of the great debate on education
   B. make it seem that Lincoln and the Constitution are on his side
   C. impress us with his historical knowledge _____

10. When Fadiman mentions the Founding Fathers in paragraphs 6 and 14, he is trying to arouse in his readers
    A. sentimental feelings for the United States today
    B. admiration for our system of education in America
    C. feelings of pride in our national heritage _____

Let's look now at *the article as a whole*, its purpose, attitudes, method, and importance or value to us.

11. The main purpose of this article is
    A. just to present us with a series of facts about education
    B. to persuade us that American education should be changed
    C. to entertain us in a light and harmless way   _____

12. In his attitudes toward education, Fadiman is
    A. conservative—he wants us to go back to the older basic education
    B. confused—he wants an assortment of contradictory things
    C. experimental—he wants us to try something entirely new   _____

13. Fadiman's method of convincing us is
    A. a slow, calm, steady accumulation of facts, facts, and more facts
    B. a mixture of fact, sarcasm, strong language, appeals to authority, and sincere pleading
    C. a confused and actually somewhat contradictory series of what appear to be random remarks

    _____

14. This article was written in 1958. Today it
    A. cannot be meaningful to us because it's an old essay
    B. is exactly as meaningful as it was in 1958
    C. is still meaningful in some ways, but not so much as when it was originally written

    _____

READING LITERATURE

Why is reading literature so different from studying a textbook? Stories, poems, essays—all are quite different from textbooks. Literature appeals more to our feeling side, textbooks to our thinking side. Literature offers special kinds of pleasure, and reveals people and problems in ways we might not understand if they were explained in a textbook.

Frederick Douglass's story of his slave days is literature. It makes us understand, better than any textbook could, how it felt to be a young slave. This kind of understanding has a unique value. College students can acquire much knowledge and many skills from textbooks, but as human beings they become more humane and civilized when they come to feel sympathy for other people and gain an understanding of their problems and hopes through literature.

That is why the study of literature is an important part of a college education—an element of growth toward maturity.

A story, a poem, an essay can give us a feeling for nature, for adventure, for family life, for beauty, for suffering, for death. Literature can open doors for us on areas of life that we might not otherwise experience, and thus can increase our understanding and appreciation of some of the most interesting possibilities of life.

As readers of literature, we must actively participate in what we read. We must hear what the people in a story say as though we were there. We must feel deep sympathy for them and their problems. Literature is human. The writers tell us of their love, their fear, their grief, their joy. We must listen to them and really hear and feel what they are saying. We must put much of ourselves and our own experience into what we read.

In the short passages that follow, you will encounter a courageous New England housewife; two young lovers meeting secretly by night; a famous man who loved the simple life of the woods; a hearty farm woman and her dinner guests; and a small boy excitedly watching two nesting birds.

READING FICTION

Our first literary passage is from a story about New England life many years ago. "The Revolt of 'Mother'" was written by Mary E. Wilkins Freeman. The situation in the story is this:

Farmer Penn didn't need a new barn, but he wanted one. For the first time his wife, Sarah, stood up to him and demanded the new house he had promised her when they were married. But he built a barn anyway. Then Sarah decided on a daring move, so daring that the storyteller compares it to a famous military action.

Farmer Penn went off to buy a horse and . . .

During the next few hours a feat was performed by this simple, pious New England mother which was equal in its way to Wolfe's storming of the Heights of Abraham. It took no more genius and audacity of bravery for Wolfe to cheer his wondering soldiers up those steep precipices, under the sleeping eyes of the enemy, than for Sarah Penn, at the head of her children, to move all their little household goods into the new barn while her husband was away. . . .

At five o'clock in the afternoon the little house in which the Penns had lived for forty years had emptied itself into the new barn.

Every builder builds somewhat for unknown purposes, and is in a measure a prophet. The architect of Penn's barn, while he designed it for the comfort of four-footed animals, had planned it better than he knew for the comfort of humans. Sarah Penn saw at a glance its possibilities. Those great box-stalls, with quilts hung before them, would make better bedrooms than the one she had occupied for forty years, and there was a tight carriage-room. The harness room, with its chimney and shelves, would make a kitchen of her dreams. The great middle space would make a parlor, by-and-by, fit for a palace. Upstairs there was as much room as down. With windows and partitions, what a house there would be!

EXERCISE 6 Answering Questions on "The Revolt of 'Mother'"

1. When Penn returned, and understood what his wife had done, he promised her the windows and furniture she needed. And he wept. Why might he have reacted

   this way?_____

   _____

2. After forty years of meekness, Sarah, the "Mother" of the story, finally asserted herself. Do you think that Mother would ever be the same again?

   Why not? _____

   _____

3. How about "Father," farmer Penn?

   _____

READING POETRY

"Meeting at Night" is a love poem by Robert Browning. A young man in a boat is coming into a cove (a small bay) and reaching land. As he speaks, we receive a series of impressions, starting with the sea, the land, and the yellow moon.

Meeting at Night

The grey sea and the long black land;
And the yellow half-moon large and low;
And the startled little waves that leap
In fiery ringlets from their sleep,
As I gain the cove with pushing prow,
And quench its speed i' the slushy sand.

Then a mile of warm sea-scented beach;
Three fields to cross till a farm appears;
A tap at the pane, the quick sharp scratch
And blue spurt of a lighted match,
And a voice less loud, thro' its joys and fears,
Than the two hearts beating each to each!

EXERCISE 7   Answering Questions on "Meeting at Night"

1. This meeting of two lovers is described by a poet, and he has his own way of describing it. In the second stanza, for example, he simply lists places and things leading to the lovers' meeting: a mile of beach . . . three fields . . . a farmhouse . . . a tap at the window . . . a lighted match . . . a voice . . . then "two hearts beating each to each." In the poem Browning is interested in
   A. short, quick impressions full of suspense
   B. careful explanations
   C. slow and deliberate storytelling   A, B, or C? _____

2. The poet wants us to share the experience of the lovers. He also wants us to see, feel and hear.
   A. Some of the things we *see* in the poem are _____

   _____

   B. In the second stanza, we *hear* _____

   _____

And we *smell* the sea-scented beach. We *feel* the prow of the boat pushing into the slushy sand. We sense the beating of the two hearts.

   Poets often want us to see and hear, feel and smell. Such sense impressions are the essence of poetry.

READING AN ESSAY

Henry David Thoreau loved Walden Pond and the woods around it. He lived there very simply, doing odd jobs for a few hours now and then to earn the little money that he needed. These "slight labors," as he calls them, were useful to society and "a pleasure" to him.

Thoreau preferred this way of life to the hustle and bustle of life in his Massachusetts town, as you can tell by these paragraphs from his essay "Life Without Principle."

> The world is a place of business. What an infinite bustle! I am awaked almost every night by the panting of the locomotive. It interrupts my dreams. There is no sabbath. It would be glorious to see mankind at leisure for once. It is nothing but work, work, work . . . .
>
> If a man walk in the woods for love of them half of each day, he is in danger of being regarded as a loafer; but if he spends his whole day shearing off those woods and making earth bald before her time, he is esteemed an industrious and enterprising citizen. As if a town had no interest in its forests but to cut them down!
>
> Perhaps I am more than usually jealous with respect to my freedom. I feel that my connection with and obligation to society are still very slight and transient. Those slight labors which afford me a livelihood, and by which it is allowed that I am to some extent serviceable to my contemporaries, are as yet commonly a pleasure to me, and I am not often reminded that they are a necessity. So far I am successful. But I foresee that if my wants should be much increased, the labor required to supply them would become a drudgery. If I should sell both my forenoons and afternoons to society, as most appear to do, I am sure that for me there would be nothing worth living for.

EXERCISE 8   Answering Questions on "Life Without Principle"

1. How did the townspeople feel about Thoreau's way of life? Did they approve? We can guess how they felt from what he says about a man who walks in the woods because he loves them. This man who loves the woods, he says,
   A. is esteemed as an industrious citizen
   B. is in danger of being regarded as a loafer
   C. spends his whole day shearing off the woods   _____

2. When Thoreau speaks of how he might "sell" both his forenoons and afternoons to society, he is talking about holding down a full-time job. According to the

   passage, what would this mean to him? _____

   _____

3. Basically, Thoreau in this passage is trying to
   A. present two different sides of the question of how he should live
   B. explain city life and life in the woods
   C. make us feel sympathetic toward his own way of life   _____

READING POETRY

Walt Whitman was an American poet who grew up loving nature. Here we see him as a boy on Long Island, which he calls by the old Indian name of Paumanok. He is watching two birds along the seashore in the nesting season.

Once Paumanok,
When the lilac-scent was in the air and fifth-month grass was growing,
Up this seashore in some briars,
Two feather'd guests from Alabama, two together,
And their nest, and four light-green eggs spotted with brown,
And every day the he-bird to and fro near at hand,
And every day the she-bird crouch'd on her nest, silent, with bright eyes,
And every day I, a curious boy, never too close, never disturbing them,
Cautiously peering, absorbing, translating.

From "Out of the Cradle, Endlessly Rocking"

EXERCISE 9   Answering Questions on This Stanza

These few lines of poetry are full of action. They are like a short play. The action takes place along the seashore in spring when the lilacs are in bloom. There are three characters, two birds and a boy. The setting is wild seashore, briars, and grass.

1. The boy is quiet and does not disturb the two birds. They are busy.

   Every day the he-bird is _____

   Every day the she-bird is _____

2. The poet wants us to feel about the birds and their nest
   A. the beauty of the scene
   B. the location of the nest in the briars
   C. the importance of the eggs to the two birds   _____

3. The boy is there, too, every day, looking and absorbing what he sees. He is also busy "translating." Here "translating" could mean
   A. watching   B. memorizing   C. understanding   _____

4. The events take place in the spring. The poet doesn't tell us this in so many words. Instead, he tells us indirectly. What two things let us know that it's spring?

   A. _____

   B. _____

5. The main feeling we have as we read the poem is for
   A. the birds, their nest, their eggs
   B. the setting: the spring, the seashore, the briars, there on Paumanok
   C. the experience of the young boy observing and appreciating the life of the the birds   _____

READING FICTION

Here is part of a story of farm life, "The Return of a Private," by Hamlin Garland. As the story begins, it's time for Sunday dinner on the farm.

At one o'clock the long table was piled with boiled potatoes, stacks of boiled corn on the cob, squash and pumpkin pies, hot biscuit, sweet pickles, bread and butter, and honey. Then one of the girls took down a conch shell from a nail and, going to the door, blew a long, fine, free blast, that showed there was no weakness of lungs in her ample chest.

Then the children came out of the forest of corn, out of the crick, out of the loft of the barn, and out of the garden. The men surrounded the horse trough to souse their faces in cold, hard water, and in a few minutes the table was filled with a weary crowd, and a row of wistful-eyed youngsters circled the kitchen wall, where they stood first on one leg and then on the other, in impatient hunger.

"Haft to eat to work," said Bill, gnawing a cob with a swift, circular motion that rivaled a corn sheller in results.

"Good land! Eat all yeh want! They's plenty more in the fields, but I can't afford to give you young 'uns tea. The tea is for us womenfolks, and 'specially f'r Mis' Smith and Bill's wife. We're agoin' to tell fortunes by it."

One by one the men filled up and shoved back, and one by one the children slipped into their places, and by two o'clock the women alone remained around the debris-covered table, sipping their tea and telling fortunes.

EXERCISE 10 Answering Questions on "The Return of a Private"

1. The farm people in this story are poor. Yet their table holds several kinds of delicious-sounding food. It lacks
   A. vegetables   B. meat   C. desserts   _____

2. There's honey from the hive, and the rest of the meal
   A. comes mostly from the fields
   B. has been purchased in town
   C. does not sound appetizing   _____

3. The hostess serves tea only to herself and the other women. This is because
   A. it's Sunday and the men haven't been working
   B. the men and children don't care for tea
   C. tea must be bought in town, and money is in short supply   _____

4. The farm woman who is hostess at this dinner works hard, in her house and in the fields. Here she seems to be
   A. depressed from hard work
   B. worried about her future on the farm
   C. hearty and cheerful in her approach to life   _____

LIBRARY SKILLS

LIBRARY RESOURCES FOR COLLEGE WORK

However large or small your college library may be, one thing is certain—it is useful. You need it for your college work.

Your number-one resource in any library is the librarian. Consider that a librarian has had a serious course of training to prepare him or her to help those who use the library. Ask questions whenever you need to. Don't, of course, expect the librarian to do your work for you. The other library resources you are likely to use are these:

The card catalogue lists the authors and titles of all the books in the library, and it also guides you to books on special topics. A call number (in the upper left corner of card) is assigned to each book, to help you locate it on the shelves.

Encyclopedias, such as the *Americana* and the *Britannica*, provide general information on thousands of subjects. Annual yearbooks help keep them up-to-date.

Dictionaries in your library will probably include some good college dictionaries, such as the *Random House College Dictionary*, or *Webster's New World Dictionary*, and others. Most authoritative, and biggest of all, is *Webster's Third New International*.

Biographical sources may include the *Dictionary of National Biography* (British to 1900), the *Dictionary of American Biography* (Americans no longer living), and, for more recent figures, *Who's Who* (British) and *Who's Who in America*. There are also *Webster's Biographical Dictionary*, *Current Biography*, which includes many portraits, and the *Biography Index*, and index to biographical material in books and magazines.

Magazines and newspapers provide up-to-date information, which is often essential for college research projects. The *Readers' Guide to Periodical Literature* is an index to the articles in the most widely read magazines. Your own library will have a list of the magazines and periodicals it subscribes to.

The *New York Times Index* will tell you that a certain event happened on April 2, 1951, or some other date in recent history, and will steer you to the issues of the *Times* that contain reports of the event. These actual issues of the *Times* will probably be on microfilm. In addition, your library may have copies of recent numbers of the *New York Times* and other newspapers, including your local paper. The *Times Index* will also help you to find the dates of important events that you want to read about in other newspapers.

Other reference works are found in even a small library. For that ever-present literature course, there's the *Oxford Companion to American* (also *English*, *French*, and *Classical*) *Literature*, as well as the handy *Book Review Digest*, which gives short accounts of many works. And there are books of quotations, atlases, world almanacs, and reference works dealing with religion, literature, science, music, or business.

Then, don't forget any special files—a pamphlet file, perhaps—that your library has. And how about records and tapes?

Learning to use the library takes *practice*. You don't learn to play tennis just by reading about it; you have to pick up that racquet and use it. The more you visit your library, the more you'll find yourself using the card catalogue and various reference tools to locate books and articles on your subject, whatever it may be.

We'll begin our library tour with some familiar stops—the card catalogue and the encyclopedia. Then we'll go on from there.

EXERCISE 1   Examining Your College Library

Your first step is to survey your own college library. What resources does it have? One that you can count on is the *librarian*. How about other resources? Tell what's available and also where it's located.

Card catalogue. There may be two of these, one for authors and titles, one for subject matter. Or there may be a single catalogue that combines both. Two card

catalogues? _____   A combined catalogue? _____

Location: _____

Where do you obtain the book you need? _____

Encyclopedias: _____

_____

Location: _____

Dictionaries: *Webster's New Third International*? Yes? _____   No? _____

College dictionaries: _____

_____

Location: _____

Biographical Sources: _____

_____

Location: _____

Magazine index: *Readers' Guide to Periodical Literature*

Location: _____
Where do you obtain the bound volume or microfilm for the article you need?

_____

Newspaper index: *New York Times Index*

Location: _____
Where do you obtain the microfilm for the article you need?

_____

Other reference works (try for those on a variety of subjects—art, religion, science, music, law, etc.):

_____

_____

_____

_____

_____

_____

<u>Let's check the location of some other library resources.</u>

Where's the desk of the reference librarian? _____

Where are the microfilm machines? _____
Where's the list of periodicals carried by your college library?

_____

Some books are placed on reserve—that is, they are set aside for use only in the library, or sometimes for overnight use. In your library, where are the books that

are on reserve? _____

Where is the newspaper rack? _____

Where is the magazine rack? _____

Where is the desk at which books are charged out? _____

Where are the fiction shelves? _____

Other notes on your library:

_____

_____

_____

_____

_____

Make a mental note that on these pages you have an account of the main resources of your college library. As you do your college work you may find these pages a handy reference of your own.

EXERCISE 2   Understanding the Card Catalogue

Using a card catalogue for a college report involves understanding the system of subject headings.

1. Select the subject heading under which you might find a card for a book on each of the topics listed below. (A bibliography is a list of books.) Write *the number of the subject heading* in the space at the left of each topic.

Subject headings	*Topics: what you're looking for*
(1) ART, ENGLISH—BIBLIOGRAPHY	_____ A. A critical study of drama in various countries
(2) ART, ENGLISH—HISTORY	
(3) ART, HISTORY	_____ B. The form of government in France
(4) DRAMA—BIBLIOGRAPHY	
(5) DRAMA—COLLECTIONS	_____ C. A book with the title *A History of Art*
(6) DRAMA—HISTORY AND CRITICISM	_____ D. An anthology of plays by English authors
(7) EDUCATION—ADULTS	
(8) ENGLAND, HISTORY. *See* GREAT BRITAIN	_____ E. A history of England
	_____ F. A list of books on English art
(9) ENGLISH DRAMA—COLLECTIONS	
(10) ENGLISH LITERATURE—COLLECTIONS	_____ G. Survey of French history from earliest times to the present
(11) FRANCE—FOREIGN RELATIONS	
(12) FRANCE—HISTORY	_____ H. History of contemporary England
(13) FRANCE—HISTORY—20th CENTURY	
	_____ I. Evening schools for adults
(14) FRANCE—POLITICS AND GOVERNMENT	_____ J. History of Negroes from the Civil War to the present
(15) GREAT BRITAIN—HISTORY	
(16) GREAT BRITAIN—HISTORY—20th CENTURY	_____ K. French-English foreign relations
(17) NEGROES—HISTORY	_____ L. Early English art

2. Sometimes more than one heading can be useful when pursuing your topic.
   A. For example, for books on Thomas Jefferson, third president of the United States, you would first look under this heading:

   _____

   B. Under what other headings might you find books that would give you further information concerning Thomas Jefferson?

   _____

   _____

221

C. Very neatly, write in the block below the information you would need to put on a library slip in order to get a book giving information about Thomas Jefferson. Be sure to include all the information you need. Copy the call number carefully.

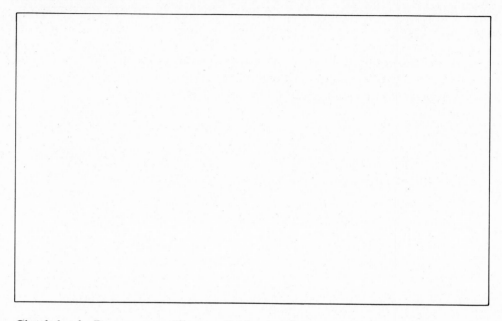

Check back. Be sure your library slip is complete.

3. For books on the United States draft system, what subject heading would you go to in the card catalogue?

_____

4. Some books listed in the card catalogue may be on reserve. How is this shown on the card for the book?

_____

5. Locate the card for a book on Franklin D. Roosevelt. The title you have chosen is

_____

   A. According to the card, how many pages does the book have? _____

   B. Does the book have a bibliography (a list of related books and articles)? _____

6. Samuel Clemens used a pseudonym, Mark Twain. Under which name is his most famous book, *Huckleberry Finn*, listed in the card catalogue?

_____

7. When working with a really current topic—something that's in the newspapers and on television *today*—what kind of information could you locate by using the card catalogue? Check one or two answers.

   A. _____ up-to-date facts.

   B. _____ background information

   C. _____ related background

EXERCISE 3   Locating Information in an Encyclopedia

Suppose that you have become an authority on some subject. You are asked to write an article on your specialty for an encyclopedia. You have a variety of information to include in your article, and you want to make it as easy for the reader to use and understand as you possibly can. So you provide *subheadings*.

Perhaps your topic is *Philadelphia*. Your subheadings could be these:

Geography	Parks and Monuments
History	Cultural Institutions
Government	Communication and Transportation
Streets and Buildings	Commerce and Industry

Now your article has been published in the encyclopedia. Ten students come to the school library needing information about *Philadelphia*. Each has a different question to be answered. Under what subheading should each student look?

The student's question is: *Subheading to look under:*

1. What is Philadelphia's most important manufactured product? _____

2. How many radio stations does Philadelphia have? _____

3. The oldest art institution in the U.S. is in Philadelphia. Which one is it? _____

4. Why is Independence Hall famous? What's the historical reason? _____

5. Fairmount Park is one of the best-known city parks. How big is it? _____

6. What was the original pattern of Philadelphia's streets? _____

7. How many council members are in the mayor's cabinet? _____

8. What style is the architecture of Philadelphia's City Hall? _____

9. What is Philadelphia's eastern boundary? _____

10. Who established the first settlement at this location? _____

Using the subheadings given in the article on Philadelphia saved the students' time. This is true of every encyclopedia article that uses subheadings.

Encyclopedias: Locating Information

For this practice, *choose two questions* from the list on pages 225 and 226. Carefully write down the name of the encyclopedia and the number of the volume you'll be using. Then copy the questions that you'll be trying to answer in the spaces provided below. Underline the key word or words.

Encyclopedia: _____ Volume number: _____

All done? Next comes your work in the library.

First, locate the volume you need. If it's not on the shelf, look around. It might be lying on a table where someone has left it, or it might be out of order on the shelf.

Next, find your article. <u>The underlined key word is your topic.</u> Be sure to pay attention to any subheadings in the article. They can help you locate the information you need.

Write your answer to each question clearly and briefly. Try to give the information in your own words so far as possible.

As you translate the information into your own words, you are fixing it in your mind. You are teaching yourself. You'll be doing this every time you look up information for a course and put it into your own words.

So be as accurate and as careful as you can. Try to use your own words.

<u>Question 1</u>: _____

<u>Answer</u>: _____

_____

_____

_____

_____

<u>Question 2</u>: _____

<u>Answer</u>: _____

_____

_____

_____

_____

_____

Check your answers before you return the volumes to the shelf.

Encyclopedias: Questions for Reference Practice

In the list that follows, the letter B means the *Encyclopaedia Britannica*. The number tells you the volume you need. B 7 would mean volume 7 of the *Britannica*. The letter A means the *Encyclopedia Americana*, and the number shows the volume.

Because editions of these encyclopedias vary, you may have to go to a volume other than the one given. Use the *index* to the encyclopedia—in the last volume. Remember to look in the article for subheadings that will help you.

Volume   Question

B 15   How is <u>milk</u> homogenized?
        What is the average rainfall on the <u>Mohave Desert</u>?

A 24   What was the 1960 population of <u>San Francisco</u>?
        What are <u>sharks</u> used for commercially?

B 18   Who was <u>Praxiteles</u>?
        On what kind of plant does <u>quince</u> grow?

A 9   What is the diameter of the <u>earth</u>?
        What are the main constituents of an <u>egg</u>?

A 4   Name four ingredients used in <u>brewing</u>.
        How were <u>bronze</u> and brass used in Indian art?

A 5   Where does the word <u>caricature</u> come from?
        What are the four kinds of still <u>cameras</u>?

A 6   How is <u>cholera</u> diagnosed?
        Where is the ancestral home of the <u>Celtic</u> peoples?

A 7   What are the climatic requirements for cultivation of <u>coffee</u>?
        What is the geological origin of <u>coal</u>?

A 9   Who was the first proprietor of <u>Dick's Coffee House</u>? When?
        When were the first synthetic <u>diamonds</u> produced?

A 10   What is the most common technique of <u>espionage</u>?
        Name two interesting features of <u>Eskimo</u> language.

B 19   What is the first step in treating <u>retardation</u>?
        What are three common materials for <u>rope</u>?

B 18   Give three kinds of symptoms of <u>psychosis</u>.
        What is the average winning hand in draw <u>poker</u>, nothing wild?

A 21   What is the most necessary information for control of <u>parasites</u>?
        Give a common nickname for <u>Philadelphia</u>.

Volume   Question

A 19   In what form did <u>Muhammad</u> deliver his message?
        Give three World War II developments in <u>military communications</u>.

A 18   In what country is child <u>marriage</u> common?
        Describe a <u>megapode</u>.

A 29   Why is Frank Lloyd <u>Wright</u> famous?
        What part of a <u>yacht</u> most affects its speed?

A 28   What two principles are important for handling prisoners of <u>war</u>?
        What is the function of vegetable or plant <u>waxes</u>?

A 27   What must a <u>typographer</u> consider in choosing his materials?
        How can you recognize a <u>vampire bat</u>?

A 8   Was the <u>costume</u> of ancient Egypt simple or elaborate?
        Is the economic importance of <u>cotton</u> small or great?

A 11   Mention two of the five types of <u>family</u>.
        How important are work buildings on <u>farms</u>?

A 12   When were the reigns of two kings from Denmark or Norway named
        <u>Frederick</u>?
        What are the two main aspects of <u>fruit</u> growing?

A 13   State simply the vegetative structure of <u>grasses</u>.
        In <u>Greece</u>, what are the most striking features of the land?

EXERCISE 4   Using Biographical Information

Biographical reference sources are constantly needed in your college work. The problem is, which one to go to? If all you want is a very brief identification, a college dictionary may be your best bet. You'll find entries such as this:

> **Jackson, Andrew**, 1767–1845; American general and statesman; seventh president of the U.S. (1829–1837); called "Old Hickory."

But for detailed information you must go elsewhere, to the card catalogue, to a reference work, or to your daily newspaper in the case of a currently prominent figure.

Page 218 mentions some common biographical sources. On page 219 you yourself have listed some of those available in your college library. While working on this page you may find others.

What source would you go to for information on each of the following people? You want enough material to write a good paragraph on the individual. You don't have time to read a book, but need only a few basic facts. For each person give a source other than an encyclopedia. Check pages 218 and 219 if you're puzzled.

1. Abraham Lincoln _____

2. The latest popular singer _____

3. The man who robbed a local bank yesterday _____

4. An American president of recent years _____

5. Ralph Bunche (black American; born 1904) _____

6. Florence Nightingale (English; died 1910) _____

7. Gwendolyn Brooks (black American; born 1917) _____

8. William Shakespeare _____

9. A recent famous scientist _____

10. The Duke of Wellington, who defeated Napoleon at Waterloo in 1815 _____

_____

When you need information on a famous person, it saves time to know where to go, what source to use. We are all dependent on encyclopedias. But it's a good idea to become familiar with other sources. If you know what your source should be—and where it is shelved in the library—you're much more likely to make good use of it.

EXERCISE 5 Using Dictionaries for General Information

Dictionaries are very useful not only for working with words but also for locating certain kinds of information quickly and efficiently.

Words—the dictionary is full of them. We tend to think of any dictionary as the final authority on words. But dictionaries don't necessarily agree. Definitions may vary somewhat. And even pronunciation is not settled. Take the word *schizophrenia*. Two pronunciations are often given:

1. skiz ə frē′ni ə   2. skits ə frē′ni ə

Some dictionaries give one pronunciation, some the other—and some give both.

Which pronunciation is given in *Webster's Third New International*? 1 or 2?_____

Now look in another dictionary or two to find the other pronunciation. Where did you

find it? In _____
Try saying the word both ways. There is a difference, isn't there?

Information—the dictionary can be a handy source. If you have a college dictionary of your own, study it and find out what kinds of information it gives.

1. A really helpful college dictionary should contain a variety of information. The purpose of this question is to help you find the dictionary that provides this variety. Look for a dictionary in your college library that lists all or most of these items. Then quickly identify each one in a few words.

    A. Alcibiades _____

    B. Bonn _____

    C. French leave _____

    D. ivory tower _____

    E. Lidice _____

    F. Passover _____

2. Suppose your English textbook (or your history textbook) says, "From the time of Chaucer's *The Canterbury Tales* all this changed." What you need to know is the date of this work.

    Your dictionary tells you this: "Chaucer, Geoffrey, 1340?–1400; English poet." But it has no mention of *The Canterbury Tales*. However, you do know now that Chaucer was an English poet. Does this help? Where would you go next to find the date of the work?

    _____

EXERCISE 6 *Readers' Guide to Periodical Literature*

The *Readers' Guide to Periodical Literature* is one of the most commonly used resources in any library. It lists alphabetically, both by subject (for example, Rock groups) and by author, articles from a variety of magazines. Bound volumes or microfilm of back issues of some of these periodicals will be available, so you can read the articles you need for your study or research. First, some preliminary practice.

One sure way to get frustrated is to try to use a reference work without knowing how. What does this mean, for example?

Stones keep rolling. E. Sanders. il Sat R 52: 67–8 N 29 '69

Well, the fact is that reference works always try to save space. So they abbreviate everything that can be abbreviated, and sometimes the result looks like gobbledygook. So what do you do? You look in the front of the book, on the opening pages, and there you'll find an explanation. For instance, here is a partial listing of the magazine titles indexed in *Readers' Guide*.

Bsns W – *Business Week*	Opera N – *Opera News*
Ebony – *Ebony*	Sat R – *Saturday Review*
Harp Baz – *Harper's Bazaar*	Sch and Soc – *School and Society*
Mod Phot – *Modern Photography*	Sci Am – *Scientific American*

Another important point: 52: 67–8 means volume 52, pages 67 and 68. You also have the title of the article, the author, and the date (November 29, 1969).

Now let's unscramble the following entries on the topic "Rock groups." (The abbreviation *il* means illustrated.)

1. Stones keep rolling. E. Sanders. il Sat R 52: 67–8 N 29 '69

   This means _____

   _____

2. The Temptations: a group in tune with the times. C. Higgins. il Ebony 26: 64–8 Ap '71

   This means _____

   _____

Headings are important in the *Readers' Guide*. Our heading here was "Rock groups." The headings in the *Readers' Guide* are somewhat similar to the subject headings in the card catalogue.

Now go to the library and actually use the *Readers' Guide to Periodical Literature*. Its most recent volumes have the highest numbers. First, look at page 231 and pick a topic that suits you.

3. Write here the topic that you'll be working on. Also note the volume number you'll be using.

_____   _____
(Topic)   (Volume number)

If there's nothing in the first volume you look at, try another. Remember, if you are working with a subject of current interest you want the latest volume of *Readers' Guide*. You might even need the paperbound issues covering the most recent months.

4. Next, copy very carefully the information you will need in order to get the bound volume or microfilm of the magazine that contains an article you want to read on your subject. Take down the information on three articles. That gives you three chances to get an article you want. (Well-known magazines, like *Atlantic Monthly*, *Harpers*, or *Ebony*, are the most likely to be in your library.)

A. _____

_____

B. _____

_____

C. _____

_____

5. Now go to the periodical desk or counter and ask for the first of the magazine articles you have listed. It it's not available, ask for one of the other articles you have listed on this worksheet. All you need is *one* article.

6. Find the article—that's easy. Look for the date and the page number you copied from *Readers' Guide*. It's the number after the colon. If the volume is on microfilm, you may need help. Don't hesitate to ask a librarian. Read or skim all or part of the article. Then give two interesting and significant facts about your subject. Use your own words so far as possible. Write carefully and accurately.

A. _____

_____

B. _____

_____

Choosing a Topic for Your Magazine Work

How should you go about choosing a topic? There are two approaches you can take.

First, you might have in mind someone or something you enjoy reading about. Do you have a favorite singer, actor, actress, sports figure? That's one kind of choice.

Second, there are subjects that are always being discussed, year after year. You'll find them listed in almost any volume of the *Readers' Guide*. Scan this list:

Witchcraft	Birth control
New York City	Diet, health
Music	San Francisco
Poverty, slums	Religion
Gangs	Urban problems
Art	Parents' concerns
Racial problems	Civil rights
War, international problems	Movies
Broadway	Hollywood
Drugs	Sexual problems
Firearms	Love
Misconduct in office	Venereal disease
Military	Psychology
Marriage	Divorce

If you select large topics like most of these, you'll probably find they have a number of subheadings. For music, you may find "Popular" and "Classical" as subheadings, and we've already worked with the heading "Rock groups." Some topics have many subheadings.

EXERCISE 7 Obtaining Information from *New York Times* Microfilm

Whether you're in New York, Atlanta, or Seattle, you are likely to hear people quote from the *Times*. This is the *New York Times*, which is sold and read from coast to coast.

In most libraries today, the *New York Times* is stored on microfilm. Since more and more magazines also are now being stored on microfilm, you need to learn how to locate information by using the microfilm reader.

So—when were you born? And what happened in the wide, wide world on that particular day? The *Times* will tell you.

The big date was _____, _____
                         (Month and date)   (Year)

Now go the libarary's magazine-newspaper counter. Ask for the microfilm that includes your date of birth. All you need to do is wind the microfilm to the front page of the *New York Times* for your date. Note the two main headlines that deal with United States or world news. What we want is the really big news for that special day.

Copy here the headlines for the two big news stories featured in the *Times* on the day you were born. Add another if there's a really interesting one.

Headline 1: _____

_____

Headline 2: _____

_____

Another interesting headline? _____

_____

Now you know what happened in the world on the day you were born. Was the news good?

RESEARCHING A TOPIC FOR A COLLEGE PAPER

Most college courses require a paper, sometimes two or more. Usually you have some choice of topic. To do a satisfactory job, you must then locate a number of pertinent sources. How do you find these sources?

The period of time involved is a major consideration. Are you interested in a topic twenty-five years old or more? Or a current topic? Each kind requires a different research approach.

If you are writing about a person or subject in the past—ten or twenty-five years ago, or several centuries ago—here are some suggestions.

General encyclopedias, the *Americana*, the *Britannica*, and others, will give you background information.

There are also specialized encyclopedias, dictionaries, and handbooks on many subjects, such as music, psychology, and science. For example, if your topic concerns Africa, look for *Africa: A Handbook to the Continent*. Among the specialized encyclopedias are the *Encyclopedia of Sports*, the *Encyclopedia of the Theatre*, the *Encyclopedia of Jewish Knowledge*, the *Encyclopedia of the Negro*, the *Encyclopedia of Islam*, the *Encyclopedia of Latin America*, and many more.

The card catalogue in your college or city library can refer you to books on your subject. Some of the books will have bibliographies, that is, lists of related books or articles that you might want to look up.

If the stacks (the shelves of books) in your library are open to students, go to the area of the stacks where you know there is a book on your topic. Look on the shelves for related books, and skim them to discover whether any will be useful to you.

Most college libraries have a reference librarian who specializes in helping students do research. Ask this librarian for special advice. You might be told there is another library nearby, perhaps your city library, where a good collection of books and other source materials on your topic are available. The librarian will also help you determine whether there are magazine or newspaper articles on your particular topic, either in your college library or elsewhere.

For a current topic—say, racial problems in South Africa today—you might still want some background sources. An encyclopedia can help you quickly review the history of your subject, and the supplementary encyclopedia yearbooks may provide some up-to-date information.

But then you must move on to current material. The *Readers' Guide to Periodical Literature* will direct you to recent articles. The *New York Times Index* will help you to locate news stories on recent and current events. Your college or city library will probably have the very latest issues of the *Times*, and other issues will be available on microfilm.

The librarian will be ready to give advice and help. After you have done all you can by yourself, go to the librarian for the advice of an expert.

LIBRARY-ASSISTED READING

A problem that is common to many textbooks is this: the writer of the text *assumes* that you are familiar with facts or ideas or names that are actually unknown to you.

Again, you must go to the library. Here it's particularly important to save time —to locate the information you need as quickly as possible.

The textbook passage that follows is typical of one kind of textbook writing. It is an introduction to a section of an anthology, a collection of poetry and prose by many authors. Since the selections themselves will illustrate the ideas discussed in the introduction, you need to grasp firmly the facts and names and ideas in such an introductory passage. The selection that follows is from *The American Identity* by Sam S. Baskett and Theodore B. Strandness.

The professor who teaches your course is undoubtedly familiar with the whole subject. For the teacher, the names and ideas and facts are everyday matters, just as they are to the textbook writer. Neither sees any difficulty in the text presentation. As for you, "If you don't know it, look it up." Here's the passage.

MEN'S WAYS WITH GOD

[1]John Milton, the great Puritan poet of England, declared his intention to "justify the ways of God to men." *Paradise Lost* was the result, a poem which justified God by showing the sinfulness of man. As the *New England Primer* put it, "In Adam's fall / We sinned all." New England and Old England differed on some important matters, such as who on this earth should rule whom, but there was general agreement concerning the nature of man. He was corrupt.

[2]In later periods God's ways with men came to seem less clear; today it is mainly concerning men's ways with God that we are able to agree. And American concepts of the Deity are various. The stern and awful God of the Puritans became, after a century or so, the remote and reasonable God of the American Enlightenment—for some of the more highly educated. A greater number of Americans, particularly those on the frontier, worshipped the God of salvation. This split between those who emphasized reason in religion and those who emphasized piety continues to the present time, although in differing manifestations. The changing ways of men with God are most strikingly seen when we compare the God of service in today's metropolitan YMCA, or the cozy Deity whom a Hollywood movie-queen termed "a livin' Doll," with their colonial Predecessor who wrathfully presided over a "bottomless gulf" of fire, hardly restrained from dropping man therein, as if he were "a spider or some loathsome insect."

[3]Beginning in the nineteenth century a note of agnostic skepticism was sounded in some American writing about God. In a poem entitled "Thought," Walt Whitman, pondering whether "souls" are "destroyed," raised the question which was to be the subject of agonized contemplation for many: "Is only matter triumphant?" Robert Ingersoll, known as the great agnostic in the 1880s and 1890s, was celebrated and reviled for his lectures criticizing the

Bible. This clash between skepticism and fundamentalism came into dramatic focus in the examination of William Jennings Bryan by Clarence Darrow at the Scopes "monkey trial" in 1925. The more searching contemporary writers on this topic, however, have abandoned both the skeptical and fundamentalist positions. And so Paul Tillich, prominent among the existentialist theologians, urges modern man to ask anew the religious question and in seeking answers to regain "the lost dimension" in religion.

EXERCISE 8   Researching Information on "Men's Ways with God"

1. Milton's *Paradise Lost* is the reference that gives us the beginning date of this discussion. The next period of time is identified only as "after a century or so." So we need to know the date of Milton's *Paradise Lost*. Find this date in an appropriate source.

   A. The date of Milton's *Paradise Lost* is _____

   B. I found this date in _____

2. The *New England Primer* is clearly an American work. If you should want to learn more about it, what would be a good source?

   _____

3. Highly educated Americans believed, we are told, in the God of the Enlightenment. If you look up this word in the dictionary, be sure to take the definition for the *capitalized* form of the word.

   A. What was the Enlightenment? _____

   _____

   B. The religion of the Enlightenment was *deism*. Benjamin Franklin, Thomas Jefferson, and many other Americans—Abraham Lincoln, for one—have been, in essence, deists. To understand the meaning of *deism*, you may need to check more than one definition. This often helps.
      For study and review purposes, there's one, and only one, kind of *good* definition of such a term—a definition written in simple words that we all understand. Study the meaning until you yourself can write such a definition. And when you've done this, you've already mastered the word.

   Now, what is deism? _____

   _____

   _____

   _____

4. We all know the general meaning of *skepticism*. We say, "Well, *I'm* skeptical," when we doubt the truth of what we hear. And we can use this general meaning for our passage. *Agnosticism* is a less familiar word. Look it up if you need to, and then try to give an agnostic's view of religion in simple words.

An agnostic believes _____

_____

5. The 1925 "monkey trial" of Scopes, we are told, focused national attention on the clash between skepticism and fundamentalism. If you wanted to find out more about this, the names Darrow and Bryan would be poor choices as reference topics because both men were involved in many other issues. Your best bet would be Scopes, since he was famous only for this one crisis. Where would you go for more information about him?

_____

6. Paul Tillich died in 1965. His influence persists. He is adequately identified here as "an existentialist theologian." A theologian is a scholar in the field of religion. But what is existentialism? That's not an easy question. Again, you'll probably need to check several definitions. Then try to write a *good* definition in the simplest words you can.

Existentialism is _____

_____

_____

_____

7. Is there anything else in the passage you need to look up? If so, give that information here.

_____

_____

_____

_____

_____

_____

_____

EXERCISE 9   Answering Reading Questions on "Men's Ways with God"

1. According to this introductory passage, there have been in the United States several views or kinds of religion. List some of the main kinds below.

    A. _____

    B. _____

    C. _____

    D. _____

    E. _____

2. "The present time" and "today" in paragraph 2 refer to the same time. What is the most exact identification we can find for "today"—the time when the authors were engaged in writing this passage? Since the book was copyrighted in 1962,

    this would probably have been the year _____

    The date when an article or book was written is often important. If we're reading about a social problem that concerns us, or a current scientific question, we want the most recent material we can find.

3. Our writers describe a number of views of religion, beginning with Puritanism. Is there any hint of a feeling of sympathy or approval in connection with the account of any of these views of religion? If so, quote below a phrase or several phrases that sound approving or sympathetic.

    _____

    _____

    Even when writers do not consciously intend to show sympathy or dislike, they may do so, perhaps just by the choice of a word.